MIND HACKING AND ESCAPING ZOMBIFICATION

How to Control Your Mind, Find Ultimate Happiness And Total Enlightenment

JAMES STEPHENSON

CONTENTS

Introduction	vii
Chapter One: Human Psychology, Behavior and How the Mind Works	1
Chapter Two: The System, Self-Limiting Beliefs and Conformation	10
Chapter Three: How Popular Narratives Build and Why Many Can't Think Beyond Them	22
Chapter Four: Is Mind Control for Real?	37
Chapter Five: Cui Bono? Who Benefits From Polarization, Hate, Unrest, Depression, War and Climate Change	49
Chapter Six: What is Critical Thinking and How Can You Develop It?	59
Chapter Seven: What Makes Self-Education, Contemplation, Focus and Taking Action So Difficult?	80
Chapter Eight: Word of Caution	93
Chapter Nine: Improving Emotional Intelligence and Self-Awareness	98
Chapter Ten: Neuroplasticity and Good Habits	115
Chapter Eleven: Staying In the Present With Mindfulness	126
Chapter Twelve: Understanding Your Inner Self With Meditation	137
Chapter Thirteen: Strategic Thinking, Decision Making and Problem Solving	144

Chapter Fourteen: Risk-Taking, Creativity and Imagination	155
Chapter Fifteen: Visualization, Affirmations and Writing Down Goals	166
Chapter Sixteen: Attitude of Gratitude	173
Chapter Seventeen: Fighting Frustration, Failures and Social Pressure	181
Final Words	189
The end... almost!	195

© Copyright 2019 - All rights reserved.

It is not legal to reproduce, duplicate, or transmit any part of this document in either electronic means or in printed format. Recording of this publication is strictly prohibited and any storage of this document is not allowed unless with written permission from the publisher except for the use of brief quotations in a book review.

INTRODUCTION

This book, *Mind Hacking and Escaping Zombification* will introduce you not only to the power of your mind but how to use it against the social and political structures that benefit the few at the expense of the many.

Are you feeling stuck in your life? Maybe you spend too much time scrolling through social media feeds. You know that's not how you're going to get what you want out of life, but it's so addicting that you find it hard to stop. Social media is addicting, by the way, and it's designed to be that way. Companies make money from selling ads to you, and they need you to spend as much time on the platform as possible so you will buy what the ads are selling.

What part of your life isn't working? Career, health,

finances, relationships? The good news is that once you unlock the secrets of how your mind works, you can use it to improve anything you wish.

Neuroscience has come a long way, especially in the past decade or so, and we know so much more about the brain as a result. There are still avenues to be explored, but scientists now understand our attention systems, how the brain responds to pleasurable stimuli, and why we can't make good decisions when we're overcome by emotion.

Companies have understood this research and learned to use it against consumers. Isn't it time you took back control of your brain and started making decisions based on what's best for you and not other people?

I explain the basics of the brain so you understand on a general level what's going on, but I'll only tell you what you need to know. This isn't a textbook full of mind-numbing (!) detail. It's a guide to the human brain, and how you can use the power of yours to create the life you've always dreamed of living.

Reading about your brain is great, but this book provides actionable steps that you can implement right away. It's important to take the steps I outline and put them into place, or else your ideal life will remain where it is now: far away and apparently out of reach. However, once you start using the skills you learn in each chapter, you'll start to see that your goals aren't so far away after all. Your mind is strong enough, but you must learn to harness its power and take control away from external actors who need you to stay in your rut.

You'll find the secrets to why you're so easily distracted, as so many of us are, and how to combat it. If you feel helpless now in front of the social, political, and commercial forces that at first glance seem so strong, you'll learn about the hacks you need to escape being helpless and take action toward your goals.

Why are these forces so strong? You'll discover who and what is the beneficiary of your learned helplessness. Not only do I teach you how to sharpen your critical thinking skills, you'll learn when they're necessary.

In addition to outside forces, some cognitive biases evolved with our brains that can keep you from achieving your dreams. I'll show you what these are and why we have them, then assist you in dealing with them. They're hardwired in so they probably won't go away, but there are ways you can counteract them.

What most people want is the freedom to live their lives in a way that makes sense to them and keeps them happy. By reading this book and putting the suggestions into place in your own life, you can reach the life you want. No matter how old you are right now, this book will show you the pathway to your dreams.

Why is this the right book for you? I'll tell you the truth. I was stuck just like you, in a job I didn't like and feeling like my life was going nowhere. I'd spend my time away from work not doing anything productive or anything that helped support my brain and happiness. I became interested in science and began keeping up with the research that started coming out about the brain.

The more I read, the more interested I grew, and I started paying less attention to video games, the idiot box (television), and social media. I learned as much as I could about how the brain works, and I read other authors who were starting to put two and two together.

INTRODUCTION

I've always been interested in the tech world, and I've always been a little cynical too. Maybe it's because I'm Gen X, or maybe it's just me, but I wasn't exactly surprised when an employee at a major social platform admitted that they'd designed their offering to trigger the addictive responses in our brains.

I had to piece things together myself to figure out how to get around these issues, to get to my dream life. How to regain control of my mind from the companies and others who want to use it against me. How to put my knowledge and experience to use, along with experts in the field, to use my mind to my advantage.

Fortunately for you, I've already been there! This book is my way to try to get as many people out of the grip of commercial zombification and lead their own lives. I've done it, and I want to share it with other people. All the information about the human brain and psychology is based on actual science.

Just remember that the sooner you start putting these steps into place, the sooner you're going to escape zombification. The sooner you start taking your mind into your own hands (as it were), rather than leaving it in someone else's, the quicker you're going to find your journey to your dreams. By contrast, the longer you take, the more zombification you'll experience.

Don't put off reading this book or deploying the suggestions. The shorter the amount of time you spend as a zombie, the better. The faster you learn the secrets to getting out of your comfortable rut, the faster you'll escape that rut. The more you take control away from the outside world and give it to yourself, the closer you'll be to your goals.

Get out before it's too late!

CHAPTER ONE: HUMAN PSYCHOLOGY, BEHAVIOR AND HOW THE MIND WORKS

The human brain is incredibly complex, as you might imagine. It evolved from our ancestors' brains, and so many of the structures that are present in our brains are also present in other vertebrate animals like lizards and cats.

The lizard brain

That's why you might have heard part of the brain referred to as the "lizard brain." It doesn't have the capacity for reasoning or rational thought. Our emotions develop here, and this is where our "fight or flight" instinct comes from.

Consider our early ancestors, living on the African Savannah. Compared to some of the other predators we weren't very big. We didn't have big scary fangs or giant claws that could be used to intimidate the other animals. Humans are not now in danger; it's the other animals that are in danger from us. However, back then the law of the jungle ruled us too: eat or be eaten.

So if there was a tiger, we had to respond quickly: fight or flee. We couldn't stand around debating with ourselves whether the tiger-shaped object was a tiger, or what we should do about it. If we didn't react quickly, we'd be eaten.

That's why, when we're under stress, the lizard brain takes over. It's a survival mechanism that has never left us, though we don't need it anymore. Still, the brain doesn't want us to stand around and get eaten. Our modern brains can't tell the difference between a true threat, like a man in a mask pointing a gun at us, and being upset because we got passed over at work for a promotion.

When our stress hormones rise and our minds perceive that we're under threat, brain function shifts to the lizard brain. Our human brain, the one that reasons and thinks and holds off on a marshmallow today because it knows it will get more in the future, is essentially turned off.

It's a resource hog, using up about 20% of our energy. It wants to be efficient. It defaults to the lizard brain anyway, which uses much less energy than the rational part of our brain. This is why brains rely heavily on heuristics (rules of thumb), stereotypes, and the like. They're much faster and easier than thinking things through and require a lot less fuel.

The rational part of the brain, which is not shared with other animals, is slow and takes much longer, using up a lot more fuel. It includes an executive function, which is how we regulate our emotions and responses. This part of the brain doesn't mature until we're 18 or 20, which is why teenagers often seem rash and reckless—their executive function is still developing.

Decision-making on purchases

Most of us prefer to believe that when we make decisions, we weigh the pros and cons of each side carefully. We rationally think through the consequences of doing A instead of B or buying X brand jelly instead of Y brand jelly. In other words, the lizard brain has taken a back seat.

It turns out that this model may be wrong. Research

on people whose emotion centers were damaged shows that they were incapable of making decisions. Other research demonstrated that the decisions arose in the subconscious before they were physically made. It's not entirely clear whether we do actually make the decision emotionally, and then retroactively figure out the rationale, as has been suggested, but we can say that emotions affect our decisions.

Emotional decisions

Many decisions in today's economy are best made based on facts. For example, whether you decide to sell all the stocks in your financial portfolio should be based on some rules you have about selling, or whether you need those stocks, not based on your emotions, which in finance tend to be either greed or fear.

However, how many people buy stocks when they're on sale or when there's been a big drop in the stock market? Almost no one, even when that's the rational action to take. No one was buying stocks in March 2009, which was the bottom of the Great Recession. Even though logic said that that was a perfect time to buy. It was too scary.

How many people sold their tech stocks during the Internet bubble? When prices were climbing higher and higher, and valuations were based on nothing but thin air? That would have been a reasonable action. But due to greed, no one did.

Advertisers and marketing firms know this. They understand perfectly well that we make decisions based on emotion. They also know that fear and greed are particularly strong triggers for purchases.

If you've ever watched a financial channel, you've seen all the ads for buying gold. It's a commodity that fluctuates in price (contrary to popular belief.) People who don't know much about stocks and commodities think it's a "safe" asset. The advertisers are banking on the fact that people are afraid of stock market drops, which are actually features of the market. No risk, no reward. But it's scary, so products that are perceived as "safe" are easy to sell.

The same companies also sell speculative investments. Bitcoin, leveraged funds (meaning that money is borrowed to increase the potential return, which also has the effect of magnifying the drops), and others are targeted toward our greed. No one's ultimate dream goals are to beat the market: people want to be able to buy a house, retire in comfort, send their kids to college. Yet advertisers urge us to buy things that will supposedly "beat the market." They taunt us to be better than boring old Jan in Accounting who only buys index mutual funds. They are investments that are all about greed.

Human conditioning

You've probably heard of the Russian physiologist Pavlov, who conditioned his dogs to associate the ringing of a bell with food. Afterward, the mere ringing of the bell caused the dogs to start salivating, even if there was no food in front of them. Although we are more complex mentally than dogs, we can be conditioned just like them.

Think about the color red, for example. When you see it on a sign, you immediately focus on it. It can mean Alert! or Danger! or simply Pay Attention! Were you born with that association? No. It's not something our ancestors in Africa evolved with, it's something that we (at least in Western cultures) have been conditioned to accept because that's the cultural significance of the color.

It's also important to note that this happens automatically. It's not something you consciously think about. You've been conditioned to it long enough that it happens without you noticing.

This can be used to your advantage, but also against you.

You can associate positive feedback with things you know you need to do, that you aren't necessarily all that thrilled about. Over time, doing those things will be associated with a good life. You'll have created a good habit that rewards you, and your brain will want you to keep doing it.

For example, suppose you know you need to get up early every morning so that you can work out, but you're not a morning person and you don't love exercising. You decide to reward yourself with a favorite podcast every time you wake up early and work out. Over time, waking up early and working out is associated with the fun podcast. You'll want to do it just so you can get your reward.

On the other hand, companies can condition you over time too if you're not careful. Social media platforms know that our brains like it when we get a notification that someone has liked and/or engaged with something we posted to our feed. If you have the platform's app on your phone (which you need to uninstall ASAP), it will give you a happy little ding noise every time this happens.

You're now conditioned to associate the little ding (buzz, vibration, however you set it) with a reaction on that platform, and you'll open up the app to see what happened. This means more time on the platform, with more time you're exposed to the ads on it, which increases the likelihood you'll buy something, even if you don't do it right on the platform.

Social media companies aren't the only ones conditioning you without you knowing it. However, they provide a very obvious example of large companies using this ability against you.

Chapter One Summary

- Human brains include portions that we share with other animals, that are the preferred default because they don't use up as much energy.
- Although we believe that we make decisions purely with logical thinking, the research shows that emotion plays a much bigger role than previously thought. Advertisers

have long known this and used it in their sales.
- Humans can be conditioned just like dogs can, and this can be used to our benefit, but also against us (as large companies have learned to do.)
- One hack: uninstall apps on your phone that give you too many needless notifications.

In the next chapter, you will learn about the System and why it's so hard to avoid.

CHAPTER TWO: THE SYSTEM, SELF-LIMITING BELIEFS AND CONFORMATION

Behavior in a society is largely based on culture and norms. While there are laws about issues like theft, murder, and wearing clothing that covers the genitals, there are many other beliefs and behaviors that rest on nothing more than societal acceptance.

For instance, it's not against the law to cut in line at the grocery store, but it's frowned upon. When you're waiting for something and there aren't any ropes or guidelines for where to stand, most people (at least in Anglo cultures) will make a line. They'll find the last person and step behind them. There's no law about this, but that's how we've been conditioned to wait when there are a lot of people somewhere.

These types of expected behaviors and norms are what make the System run so smoothly.

What is the System?

The System is the total of the culture that tells us how to behave, including governments and other authority figures, corporations, churches, and other institutions that would prefer we behave a certain way; the spoken and unspoken norms.

The System in the US tells us that if we perform well at school, then go to college and then get a good solid job, we will be rewarded with a nice house, a spouse, some children, decent salary, and then a comfortable retirement. The System doesn't want us thinking too much about mortality, or whether the System itself even works—which it no longer appears to do, at least for the vast majority of Americans. The System now only works for the wealthy or those with wealthy connections.

Otherwise, the only way to go through college is with massive amounts of debt that you'll still be saddled with decades later. The nature of work has changed, and very few companies are hiring people for full-time jobs that come with healthcare and a retirement package, leaving recent grads scrambling to cobble together jobs to make enough money to afford a place to live and something to eat.

And yet, well-meaning parents still watch out for their kid's grades, to make sure they're good enough to get into college. The kids also are shepherded to music classes and organized sports and other organizations to show the colleges that they're "well-rounded." Some of these parents are still saddled with college debt themselves! Why do they do so, when it's clear they're just passing debt down to the next generation?

Indoctrination starts early...

What kind of behavior is rewarded at elementary school? The ability to sit quietly and focus on one task at a time. Coloring outside the lines is frowned upon. Excessive fidgeting, running, or other movement is likely to be punished. Even though kids need a lot of physical activity, the school districts have cut back on recess (and other non-academic subjects like art and music) to teach to the tests.

The tests have nothing to do with whether the individual child's needs are being met. They're done to make sure that the US stays competitive with other countries in certain areas, like science and reading.

Yes, we need a literate population, for various reasons, but money might be withheld for underperforming schools in a district if not enough kids pass the tests. Salaries might be reduced—for the teachers, not the administrators.

Meanwhile, the kids are also taught the norms: sit down, but sit up straight, don't talk back, and only ask questions when the teacher says it's okay. If you're a good little boy or girl, the teacher or authority figure will like you, and that's how you get a good life.

... and it doesn't stop

Into high school, college, and beyond, the conforming students are the ones who are rewarded. The ones who don't talk back, don't get in trouble, don't get up and run around when they feel like they desperately need to get out of their chairs. Following the rules is what gets you into a good college, where you're expected to follow the rules of the authorities too.

In college, you have more freedom, because at least your parents aren't around. You schedule your classes, and no one will say much if you skip class.

Though you're warned that's the way to failure and lack of a degree.

There are usually required classes that you have to take to graduate, some kind of core curriculum. Unfortunately, these aren't usually life skills like how to manage your retirement investments or spend within your means.

Once you graduate, you get a job where you follow the boss's rules. No matter how arbitrary or counter-productive, as long as you follow them you'll get your 2% annual salary raise. Depending on where you work, you might have several layers of management, and therefore several layers of rules, to deal with.

Societal norms and acceptance

Now that you're making money, you're expected to find a spouse and then the two of you to buy a house together. If you live in an apartment, you may be punished by the tax code (though at least you miss some of the costs of homeownership.) If you don't have a spouse by the time you're in your forties, the unspoken assumption is that there is something very wrong with you. Especially if you're a woman, though never-married bachelors aren't exactly welcome either.

Once you're married, you're then supposed to have children. The correct number varies over time, though recently it seems to have landed on two. One ends up a spoiled brat, but three is too many and contributes to overpopulation. If you are married and don't have any children, that's acceptable only if one or both of you are infertile. And even then it's more embarrassing than acceptable. On the other hand, if you're not married and you have children, then that's even worse!

When you think about these expectations, who enforces them? There's no law that you must be married at least once by the age of 40. Having two children after marriage isn't a legal requirement. Certainly, corporations focus on happy, two-parent families with appropriate numbers of children in their advertising and support this ideal.

So, who is it? It's other people. Probably your parents, as anyone who's over 30 and isn't married or doesn't have children can attest. Friends maybe, the leader at the church. Everyone on social media who lambastes single mothers, or makes fun of someone who isn't married, or rips on a three-child family.

While it's just other people, and many of us have been told not to care about other people... these norms seem pretty strong. Many infertile people won't discuss it because of the shame. There's nothing logically shameful about not being able to have children, especially since there are a lot of people who experience it, but the societal expectations are so heavy that it's not something they want to discuss.

Consider how unmarried people, especially women, are shunned. Since all women are expected to be focused on having a husband, everyone assumes that if you bring an unmarried woman to a dinner party she's going to prey on the men so she can get one herself. Unmarried men are slightly more acceptable, but they get the side-eye too.

Humans are social animals. Social ties for us are linked to longer lives. Having a strong social network can provide physical immunity against viruses. The threat of taking away that support is a very powerful punishment for many people. That's why, even when we're unhappy, some might choose to stay in their rut, for fear of losing out on these community benefits. Even for those who are more willing to take a different path, it may still be hard to walk away from their current bonds.

Self-limiting beliefs

These are assumptions about how the world works and your place in it, that prevent you from achieving your goals.

Suppose you're in an unhealthy marriage. You're reluctant to get a divorce because your friends will no longer be your friends after the divorce. You'll be lonely and left without support. Although you're miserable because your marriage isn't working, you think that you're better off staying so you can keep your social network.

In this example, you are probably not wrong that you'd lose friends. You might not lose all of them, but you would lose some of them. However, what if I told you that you could make new friends? After all, there are plenty of people in this world that have been divorced. It's highly unlikely that all of them would avoid you for something they have been through! The self-limiting belief here is that you would be left without support. If you knew that you would make new friends and eventually not feel so lonely, you'd leave your unhappy marriage.

Lack of self-confidence and self-worth

Our beliefs about the world are how we make sense of it, starting in childhood. However, they're not facts, which means they're not necessarily true. People with parents who abused substances often end up believing that they're worthless because their parents chose booze or drugs over them. Others had parents without much money who worked very hard to keep them clothed and fed, but they weren't home very much and their children might believe they're not lovable.

Kids who don't do well in school might grow up thinking they're stupid, or that they'll never succeed, when in fact they were just a little hyperactive, or the style of teaching didn't gel with the way they learn best. Even those who weren't punished and had well-meaning parents can end up with inaccurate beliefs. Parents who want their kids to do well so they can get into the right schools and get on that success treadmill often end up doing their child's work. Then the child believes they're incompetent or unable to do anything difficult.

And so on. Once we form beliefs, they're hard to get rid of. Even if they're not an accurate assessment of how the world works, it's no surprise that so many people remain in their ruts, because they simply don't believe that they can climb out. It's safer (and easier, let's be honest) to stay in the societal cocoon.

Self-limiting beliefs continue right on into adulthood. You might see a job posting and think you don't have enough experience, so you don't apply, and obviously, you don't get the job. Your belief about the amount of experience necessary might have prevented you from getting a decent job, but the reality is that everyone has to start somewhere. Entrepreneurs often don't have a lot of experience in their field before they dive right in!

Who benefits from self-limiting beliefs? Not you, because you'll never lead your dream life when you don't try anything because you already believe you can't do it. The System benefits, though. They need people to conform, to stay in their jobs because they have to pay for the mortgage.

The System doesn't need a bunch of people who are doing what they want to do and achieving their goals. It does need some. Paradoxically, a few iconoclasts demonstrate to people who don't look very closely that the System does work. However, most people need to remain on that treadmill, to stay yoked to their boring corporate jobs to pay the mortgage and feed the kids and buy the cars they're sold. To use the money people earn from their boring jobs to get away on vacation periodically, preferably to a resort run by another corporation.

When you come up against a limiting belief, ask yourself if it's true. In the earlier example, you could ask yourself if it's true that you would have no support once you divorced. If you're not sure, you can try searching for groups that you might find helpful. Such as divorce recovery groups. Once you can see concrete evidence that your belief isn't true, it will help you to discard it.

In later chapters, we'll discuss how to deal with these types of beliefs, and to create a plan for escape.

Chapter Two Summary

- The System is made up of all the institutions that support the consumer treadmill.

- Indoctrination into proper behavior starts in childhood and continues into adulthood.
- Societal norms reinforce the notion of proper behavior and keep people from breaking those norms by the threat of removing social networks. These are extremely important to social animals like humans.
- Beliefs are how we understand the way the world works, and how we work in that world. They become self-limiting when they prevent us from reaching our own goals.
- One hack: when you come across a self-limiting belief, try to find out if it's true.

In the next chapter, you will learn about how the popular narrative is enforced and why it's so hard to think beyond it.

CHAPTER THREE: HOW POPULAR NARRATIVES BUILD AND WHY MANY CAN'T THINK BEYOND THEM

The American economy has changed over time, and that's influenced popular culture in addition to the rise of computers and digitization. In the early years of its founding, the country was mostly agricultural. As the Industrial Revolution hit the shores of the US, more mechanization eventually led to the transition to a manufacturing economy. After World War II, manufacturing was a big sector of the economy, which kept growing, roughly until the 1970s.

In the 1970s and 1980s, world economies became more tightly linked, for better or for worse. Manufacturing was mostly based on oil, so the oil shocks in the 1970s had a profound effect on the US. America went off the gold standard and currencies began to float, though most tethered to the dollar.

More exports started arriving, especially from Asian countries. Japanese cars began to compete.

Products made in other countries tended to be cheaper, and American companies started outsourcing their manufacturing. It kept prices down and American consumers buying. In a few decades, the US transitioned from a manufacturing economy to a consumer one.

Credit cards became more popular as regulations changed. Previous to the 1980s the most popular purchase plan was called "layaway." Shoppers could set aside an item they wanted, pay in increments over time until they had paid the purchase price and then receive the item. The influx of buy now, pay later credit cards was and is more attractive for shoppers. Unfortunately, it's usually worse for them financially. However, it fits in well with a consumer economy.

Attention economy

We've almost moved beyond a consumer economy at this point, but not quite. People still shop, using credit to buy items that they might not even need. However online, the advertising competition for consumers isn't as much for products as it is for attention.

Online media, whether it's social or otherwise, needs your attention for as long as possible so that you'll see as many ads as possible. The media itself is neutral: it doesn't care whether you end up buying shoes, cleaning products, clothes or toys from its advertisers, just that you buy something from them. To put enough ads for long enough in front of your eyeballs, the media has to command your attention for long enough to buy.

Your attention is limited, as is everyone's. Media and advertisers are competing for a limited resource. The time you spend on one platform, and the attention you give to one platform, is by definition time and attention you're not paying on another. Competition is fierce, so everyone competing for your attention is using the latest and best neuroscience research to try to keep you on their channel.

How companies compete for your attention with science

Recent advances in neuroscience provide marketers with the tools they need to leverage your mind into buying their products. What we now know is that much of the brain-body communication is done with chemicals and electricity. The function of chemicals known as neurotransmitters is to send signals from neurons (nerve cells) to whatever their specific target cells are. The neurotransmitters attach to their specific receptor on the target cell, and that triggers the target into action.

One of the neurotransmitters is a "pleasure chemical" known as dopamine. It coordinates muscle movement and helps in memory and learning. Not having enough dopamine can cause depression as well as Parkinson's disease. Because humans need certain amino acids to be able to produce dopamine, a healthy diet with enough protein is key.

When dopamine is released, the brain is basically saying, I like this. Let's do more of this. (Which can lead to addiction if left unchecked.) It's not so much a reward in and of itself, but it signals the brain to find rewards. In other words, dopamine is the key to motivation.

The brain has evolved to be attracted to new things. Brand spanking new things, not just things that are slightly different from what it's seen before. When it sees something new, it releases dopamine. It's saying, go find more of that. Each little stimulus is a prod to explore more because the brain expects a reward. It's thought that novelty can help us learn, because of this motivational aspect.

However, this type of motivation is also used to try to capture our attention on any given platform. When your phone or other device emits a signal that you've received a notification, there's a little dopamine release. That's part of the reason people end up glued to their phones. They're conditioned to check the notification because apps are designed to provide some reward for it.

Animations, whether it's a video or a GIF, attract our attention too. We've evolved to keep an eye on movement. Leaping tigers are dangerous, and the ancestors who paid attention to their movement and fled are the ones who survived, passing that trait down to us. They also tend to light up the novelty-seeking centers in the brain.

Another tactic is simply to prevent access to the app that the user wants until they've seen the ad. Currently, it seems like nothing is available to watch on YouTube unless you sit through the ad first. And of course, the ad you're sitting through has been targeted to you specifically.

Using algorithms to target ads

The rise of massive computing power has enabled companies to make assumptions about what you'll like, based on the things you've already liked, or on how long you spent looking at a previous ad plus the buying behavior of people similar to you in some way.

Before knowledge of algorithms was well-known to the general public, companies were using them even for direct mail advertising. A large company churned through its massive amounts of data and discovered buying patterns for women who were pregnant, but very early on in the pregnancy. Not obvious things like cribs, but some nesting behavior that occurred even before family members had been told about the pregnancy. When the company saw these buying patterns in its consumers, it then sent them inserts for baby products in its weekly ad flyers.

This ended up freaking out the consumers because sometimes the rest of the household didn't know what was going on! The company had to stop sending out the ad inserts due to the pushback. However, it shows you how powerful these algorithms can be.

Booksellers and video-on-demand companies discovered this trick. That's why after buying a book or seeing a show, you'll see something that says "If you read book X, then you'll love book Y!" or a list of recommended shows to watch because you liked show Z. They're open about it, but not all companies are.

Keeping you in your bubble

Algorithms aren't just used for direct selling, they also play on our confirmation bias to keep us on that channel or platform. This bias is hardwired into our brains, probably to keep us moving forward instead of constantly looking back and debating whether we made the right decision.

Confirmation bias pushes us to avoid changing our minds. Whatever decisions we've made in the past, it removes or discounts all the negative or contrary evidence. We remember the good reasons for the decision and forget or minimize the others. That's why hindsight is 20/20! In retrospect, the choice we made was the right one.

It also prevents us from spending too much time studying evidence or reasons that go against our beliefs, so that our view of the world is confirmed to be the right one. Before algorithms and cable TV channels, Americans could only watch a handful of TV stations. All of them reported similar items and tried to stay above politics. In that world, there were agreed-upon facts. You might not like them, but there they were.

Obviously, that's no longer the case. Our brains like being right. To keep us on their platforms, online algorithms are designed to feed us the information we'll like. Therefore, the information will likely confirm our worldview, which we find pleasurable, sticking around and giving their advertisers plenty of time to get their targeted ads in front of our eyeballs.

The algorithms are content-neutral and don't need to be factual. If you believe in a flat earth, in defiance of every branch of science and accumulated centuries of knowledge, the algorithms will still find as much flat-earth backup as they can. Whether the content comes from conspiracy theorists or wherever you'll see it in your feeds. A happy flat-earther is a happy consumer.

The algorithms will serve up like-minded people and content, even for morally repugnant beliefs. Those who hold beliefs may come to believe that more people agree with them than not, which can be dangerous to others.

Social media distraction

Thinking requires work on our part. As noted earlier, the thinking, rational part of our brain is newer in evolutionary terms. It's slow and it takes up lots of fuel, which our brains don't like. Because it is so much slower than the lizard brain, deep and complex thinking takes time, uninterrupted time, where rational thinking can take the time and resources it needs to puzzle through something.

Online media, and social platforms especially, seriously interfere with this "Deep Work." Research has shown it doesn't matter what the distraction is. The fact that there's any interruption at all sets the thinking machine back. It takes nearly half an hour to recover from an interruption. The same study demonstrates that on average, people lose about 2 ½ hours of productive work a day due to these interruptions. That's about 70 hours a month.

Seventy hours a month that you're not thinking. Much of that time now is likely spent on social media, so during much of those hours you're being exposed to ads that are specifically designed not to confront you with facts you don't want or opinions you don't care for.

By the way, 2 ½ hours of that 70 was at work. How much time do you spend scrolling through online feeds instead of working? That's even more time to expose yourself to ads.

Social media especially gives us the superficial feeling that we're connected. We're social animals, so that should be good, right? It does help us stay in touch with far-flung family and friends. But that kind of communication is no substitute for face-to-face interaction (which our brains still prefer) or even being on the phone with someone. Unless you're directly interfacing, it's not the same kind of communication that's so crucial to our survival.

The bigger problem is that we're missing out on face-to-face and phone calls due to our reliance on tech. We know social media makes us lonelier. The more time we spend on it, the lonelier we get, and also less able to think critically about what's happening. The constant distractions from notifications don't help, either.

One way to combat all of this is to disable all the app notifications on your phone. Stop being distracted and mind-gamed.

Lack of critical and free thinking

To capture our attention, so their advertisers can sell us things, the online infrastructure is designed to keep our minds happy by playing to our biases. Whatever they may be.

Before social media, you might have been forced to confront information that contradicted your worldview. For example, if you believed that civil rights weren't important, you'd still see television coverage of marches and speeches by thousands of people that indicated the opposite. Some people might still choose to ignore what they saw, but others might think about what they'd seen and consider whether they were wrong. Those who believed in a flat earth would still see the picture of the moon landing, with a (clearly not flat) earth off in the distance.

In other words, people sometimes had to ask themselves if they were wrong.

MIND HACKING AND ESCAPING ZOMBIFICATION

No one has to do that anymore. And many people don't want to. Our brains like being told they're right. It doesn't matter what the source of the information is, confirmation bias is confirmation bias.

Why investigate the source? If you believe in a flat earth and someone agrees with you, it's just a buzzkill to find out that the person who agrees with you is currently taking up space in a mental institution and will never leave, or that the source is someone who believes in every conspiracy theory that's currently circulating, including some that you think are completely ridiculous. No, they've confirmed your belief, and there's no reason to go poking around for their background.

Combine this with the educational indoctrination to the System, as previously discussed. Schools aren't teaching independent thinking, they're teaching to the test. Random questions are just interruptions in the lesson plan of the day. Not only is no one being taught how to think critically for themselves, they're growing up in an online world that is designed to justify whatever thoughts they have.

Thinking critically also means being critical of the System itself, which it's not exactly designed for. It's not that there's a big conspiracy between governments, institutions and online media to keep people happy and uncritical. It's more that as all these structures grew together, the benefits intertwined with each other.

That's how the popular narrative develops, and why it's so hard to step out of it. Almost everything you encounter, online or off, is designed to get you to buy something. Some baby clothes, a pair of shoes, water with lots of calories so you can be just like your favorite athlete without getting off the sofa, a public figure's philosophy so you'll donate to them. Online channels support all of this buying behavior with content-neutral algorithms that keep your brain happy and unthinking.

Chapter Summary

- Over time the US economy has shifted from an agricultural to manufacturing to consumer-based society, and the online economy is based on attention to support the consumer economy.
- The increase in knowledge about the brain

has led to ways in which companies can use our brain chemistry against us.
- Massive computing expansion led to very precisely targeted algorithms, so companies can keep you on their platform longer and get more ads in front of you.
- The shift to the attention economy has made us lonelier and less able to think critically and freely.
- One hack: turn off all app notifications.

In the next chapter, you will learn whether mind control is real.

A Short message from the Author:

Hey, are you enjoying the book? I'd love to hear your thoughts!

Many readers do not know how hard reviews are to come by, and how much they help an author.

I would be incredibly thankful if you could take just 60 seconds to write a brief review on Amazon, even if it's just a few sentences!

>> **Click here to leave a quick review**.

Thank you for taking the time to share your thoughts!

Your review will genuinely make a difference for me and help gain exposure for my work.

CHAPTER FOUR: IS MIND CONTROL FOR REAL?

In the 1950s and 1960s with the Cold War still raging, claims of alien sightings increased or were at least popularized. The lizardmen were taking over! The Russians/Chinese/Communists were implanting chips in our brains! All kinds of conspiracies about controlling the American mind arose—reptilians, aliens, Russians, maybe even the US government.

Conspiracies are largely fiction, and they tend to reflect the anxieties of the world in which people are living at the time. However, the fact that (as far as we know) lizard people are not arriving to take over our minds does not mean that we're completely free of attempts to meddle them in one way or another.

Cold War

Fears about mind control started with "brainwashing" as Communists in other countries were popularly supposed to be taking control of the minds in their countries. Some American servicemen were so horrified by what they had done in North Korea that they didn't want to return home. What else but brainwashing could account for this?

Movies like "Invasion of the Body Snatchers" and "The Manchurian Candidate" played on these fears. "Thought control" was popularly imagined to be incredibly powerful. So powerful that the military-industrial complex needed to combat this Communist brainwashing with... good old-fashioned American brainwashing.

The CIA experimented with LSD and other thought-control experiments beginning in the 1950s, not very long after it had first been synthesized by a German researcher. The experiments continued for about a decade. The CIA attempted to destroy the records during the Watergate scandal. However, a Freedom of Information Act (FOIA) request filed in 1977 brought up Project MK-Ultra.

In the project, the CIA tested all different kinds of people, not just agents, and many of them without consent. They tested LSD in addition to sleep deprivation and other methods of thought control.

The precedent was set for brainwashing experiments on unwilling participants here in the US.

The "idiot box"

Television also became popular during the early years of the Cold War. For many years, most Americans had three channels available, plus some public service channels, until roughly the 1980s when Fox and cable arrived. During the heyday of TV, no one at those channels thought that the news should make money. The news was a public service.

In the 1980s, media companies began buying each other and forming huge conglomerates that were responsible to their shareholders. Now, the news wasn't a public service. News was part of a public company that was expected to deliver value ($$$) to its owners. One way to show a better bottom line is to cut costs. News budgets were slashed, and the quality of their reporting downgraded too.

This occurred pretty much at the same time as the large organizations had better access to demographic data. They could slice and dice their advertising and target one niche or another. Cable TV appeared and they were able to target niches too, so the same version of the news was no longer available no matter which channel you were on. No longer a public service or an important asset to TV, the news became commoditized.

Cable also required that content be available 24/7, and relied heavily on breaking news. Reporters had much less time to fact check their stories and sometimes had to rush to air. The combination of more ads and dumber content led to television sometimes being known as "the idiot box".

Ads on TV, online or in the movies are much more immersive than in print. The human brain is attracted by novelty, and moving pictures are far more interesting than an ad just sitting there on a piece of paper not doing anything. People still watch TV ads, and they still buy things they see on their idiot boxes.

TV advertisers have long studied the American psyche. They know what gets us to buy—it's all emotional, with fear and greed being the most powerful purchase triggers. They can combine the power of the box with the power of using their knowledge of human nature, for a potent way to influence American consumers to keep consuming.

Smartphones

We know that the electromagnetic radiation from cellphones can interrupt or interfere with airplane controls and hospital equipment. Can it affect our brains as well? Though some believe that the radiation physically affects them, no research has shown this in a lab experiment.

Of more concern is the content found on smartphones. Companies use data to try to steer our thoughts. Every notification has a purpose, which is not really to let us know that something occurred. It's to bring us back to our phones. To spend more time on our phones.

Think of all the data on your phone—all the websites you browse, all the things you buy, all the forums you visit. There is a wealth of information about you available from this data. The more you look at your phone, the more data you're providing. The more time you spend on your phone, the more the advertisers are in front of you.

Remember how good it feels for your brain to anticipate rewards? Smartphones play into that. Many people are unaware that these techniques are being used against them on the very devices they take to bed with them. (Don't take your phone to bed. Leave it to charge in a different room.)

Don't allow the smartphone makers to get you addicted to their products.

Social media

The discussion of smartphones leads right into social media since they are creating a lot of the content that's controlling your actions. If you feel compelled to look at your phone every time you get a notification, you've now been conditioned by the social media companies. They want you to be addicted to their product.

Sound far-fetched? They've actually admitted to it. In fact, major players at Facebook don't use it themselves and won't allow their children near it. Tim Cook of Apple won't let his kids on social networks either. The true audience of Facebook and other social media networks isn't the user. After all, we get on for free! The audience is advertisers, and they're buying our attention.

The reason we refresh our screens (or they refresh for us, on some social media channels) is due to that hardwired desire for novelty. The more a network can provide us with the novelty, the longer we stay on it. What you need to understand is that none of this happened by accident.

Social media is designed to be addictive. They understand as advertisers do, how we react to novelty and intermittent rewards. Like rats, we'll keep pushing that lever if we know that from time to time we'll be rewarded. The social media channels specifically design their notifications and their underlying structure to keep us pushing that lever. The longer we push it, the longer their true audience has time to get in front of us.

Have you ever been to a casino? They don't have windows or clocks, because they don't want you remarking on the passage of time. If you did, you might remember that you have other things to do! Instead, they've got flashing lights, beeps and exciting noises that appeal to the brain's love of novelty. The longer they can keep you in the casino, the more money you'll spend. Social media networks use the same basic principles. Because they work.

Designers of apps don't present things as a page (like Google does) because then you'd have to actively choose to move on to the next page. They don't want you to make those decisions. Instead, the bottom of the screen just keeps unrolling, without you doing anything but waiting to see what happens next.

Think the "like" button is innocuous? It too is designed to harness our dopamine reward system. It reinforces our need for social validation, as well as our "score." We need to know where we are in the social hierarchy because we're social animals and "scores" and "ratings" feed that need. It's the same reason people play video games, jonesing to reach a high score on the machine or game.

Are video game, app and social media developers actually implanting anything in our brains to control us or to control our minds? No, of course not. But what they are doing is using our knowledge of how the brain works against us, in the service of their advertisers.

Surveillance state

Similarly, although we are being surveilled more than we know and often not with our freely given consent, no one is actively taking control of our minds. However, the state is creating knowledge bases that are far more detailed and invade our privacy.

Some people say that it's fine to surveil people if those people have nothing to hide. This is a naive take, at best. The issue is that even if you have done nothing wrong, you could either be swooped up in a group of people who are suspected of doing something wrong, or someone who doesn't like you can use the surveillance state against you and for the most part there's nothing you can do about it.

> "One reason is that yesterday's extreme cases often become today's standard practice." - Pierre Lemieux

Surveillance is dangerous in its way of creeping up on us. We're searched, or "inspected" at checkpoints. Border agents are free to look into your smartphone (and other devices) without even so much as a warrant. NSA spies on Americans that get caught up in its net, even though it's "supposed" to be spying on foreign nationals, not us. The FBI has about as many DNA records on the American population as the Chinese do on theirs... even though they're popularly known as an autocratic regime.

With all this information, the government has more control over its population, in terms of new laws and regulations. They're less costly to implement with the data that's gathered. You might end up violating a law that you didn't know about and with all the information the government has, they can find you pretty easily!

As new technologies come online, they're employed by the government as well as their contractors to add more surveillance, tools such as facial recognition, AI and iris scanners. The ability to collect massive amounts of data and to use behavior prediction software is used against the citizens.

One of the problems with the software is one that was ground into every programmer's brain in the 1980s: garbage in, garbage out. Some of these algorithms are hidden, and AI means that the machines "learn" in a way that can't necessarily be tracked, but if the wrong populations are used for the learning, the algorithms end up reinforcing racial and ethnic bias. Then the companies claim there's nothing they can do, because it just came out of the machines, even though they fed the algorithm garbage in the first place.

For example, a popular facial recognition software matched 20% of California senators with actual criminals. Now, you may believe that some of the work senators do is criminal, but it's not illegal, and the facial recognition software believed that the senators were the same as people behind bars for illegal activity. Imagine being matched with a criminal by software and you don't have the money to prove you're not that same criminal.

Some of this tracking occurs on your phone. The very smartphone that has been designed to be addictive, so you spend all your time on it, also has trackers and bots that know where you are at any given time. Our calls, emails and shopping habits are monitored by the surveillance state which then makes assessments about how much of a threat we are at any given moment. All this information is being fed into modeling systems to predict whether we're about to commit a crime. Yes, Orwell's thoughtcrimes are pretty much here.

Chapter Summary

- Brainwashing was originally believed to be a tool of the Communist state, but the US

government began to investigate it for its own use.
- Television began to broadcast to narrow niches and allow their advertisers to target consumers more closely.
- Today's technology is designed to be addictive, so the designers try to keep you on their platforms as long as they can in order to keep you in front of the advertisers.
- The surveillance state is also doing its part to control the population.
- One hack: be careful about what you share on social media.

In the next chapter, you will learn about who benefits from the modern world's apparent chaos.

CHAPTER FIVE: CUI BONO? WHO BENEFITS FROM POLARIZATION, HATE, UNREST, DEPRESSION, WAR AND CLIMATE CHANGE

All of this mind control and zombification doesn't just happen, leading us down the road to destruction. There's money behind it. From companies that benefit from stealing our attention to those that benefit from people staying blind to threats like climate change.

Profit at the expense of humanity and the environment

Unfortunately for Mother Nature, there's very little money to be had in keeping parts of the earth clean, green and conserved. Parks don't make very much money, but drilling for oil does. So does fracking. This innocuous-sounding name belies the damage done by the procedure. If you're not familiar with hydraulic fracturing, it's a method that allows companies to access natural shale gas and oil deep in the ground. You inject a mix of sand, water, and other chemicals at high pressures inside a well, which breaks apart the shale rock beneath the surface.

Fracking has made the US less dependent on foreign oil sources such as the Middle East and Russia. Burning gas doesn't have the same environmental impact, at least in terms of carbon dioxide air pollution, like oil and coal.

However, injecting toxic chemicals into the wells has the effect of poisoning groundwater. Although the process doesn't release as much carbon dioxide, it can release other chemicals like methane and benzene, which are also air pollutants. Because so much water is needed to increase the pressure, areas around fracking sites might even experience droughts. That isn't just a problem for the land, but also for the people, plants, and animals that depend on the land.

Relying on fracking instead of focusing research on renewable energy means that we're still burning fossil fuels and contributing to global warming.

Obviously, the fossil fuel companies benefit from

destroying the environment. The Koch brothers and other large foundations support climate denial. Politicians who are owned by fossil fuel companies benefit hugely from rolling back environmental regulations.

There's also a very large overlap between people who benefit from destroying the land and those who benefit from ignoring the rest of humanity. Let's face it, the rich don't get richer by caring about people who have less than they do.

In fact, the wealthier you are, the less generous you are. Poor people, who depend on others to get through during the hard times, are shown to be less selfish than those who have plenty of money to distribute. Perhaps, as a result, they tend to be more empathetic and more emotionally connected to other people. So if you think the wealthy are stingy and selfish... you're right. They steal more often than poor people do, and act unethically more often as well. Need proof? Check out the string of grifters in prominent positions in the 2016-2020 White House administration.

Companies that are involved in businesses that don't rely on the good of humanity tend to do better. The military-industrial complex (more about them later) makes a lot of money, as does the fossil-fuel industry... as do other industries like alcohol, tobacco, and gaming. The VICE mutual fund invests only in "sin" stocks such as these, and cumulatively has outpaced the S&P 500 stock return since inception. Meanwhile, do-gooder stocks, socially responsible funds, and others lag the overall index.

What does that tell you about what the stock market values and what companies will do well over time?

When the people are worried about whether they're going to have enough money for their mortgage payments, or whether they need to ration their lifesaving medicine because they can't afford it, they're not rioting in the streets or calling their political representatives. They're putting their heads down and working.

They don't have much time to relax, and they feel stressed and overworked, so they settle in front of the idiot box or their computer screen and allow companies to determine what they see and what's attractive to them. By the way, the only developed country where people have to ration medicine because they can't afford it is the United States. All the others have figured out health care for their citizens.

Warfare

Believe it or not, there was a time even as late as the 20th century when the US military fought its own wars, back when we had the draft. Defense jobs were done in-house, by career defense employees. Not just the military is involved in American defense, but also civilian agencies such as the Central Intelligence Agency (CIA) and Department of Defense (DOD).

The rise of alphabet soup agencies such as the National Reconnaissance Office (NRO) and National Security Agency (NSA) has come in tandem with the political Right's insistence on paring down the federal government and giving more business to private companies, which has not resulted in increased efficiencies or lowered costs. Instead, it's increased the paychecks of people like Erik Prince, who is CEO of Blackwater, a large defense contractor, whose sister, despite having no education qualifications whatsoever, currently heads up the Department of Education.

Secret defense spending, largely under the rubric of

national security, has skyrocketed, and the contractors are raking it in, reporting it on their analyst conference calls. Lockheed Martin, for example, expects their share of "restricted" money to grow to $1 billion this year, and Raytheon has absorbed $7 billion. Northrop Grumman, who earned about $1 billion from these activities in 2018, expects that portion of its revenues to grow faster than the unrestricted business.

What are they doing with the taxpayers' money? We don't know—it's "classified". Who else is benefitting from all of this money, other than shareholders? Most of whom are already wealthy? After all, 84% of stocks are owned by the top 10% of households. The others who benefit are the politicians they purchase, of course. All that revenue makes a hefty contribution to making sure that the spigot stays open.

What exactly is the military-industrial complex? It's the alliance between a country's armed forces and its defense contractors. The dangers were known as far back as 1961, when President Dwight D. Eisenhower —himself a military man, before he became president—warned against it in his farewell speech upon departing the White House.

"In the councils of government, we must guard against the acquisition of unwarranted influence, whether sought or unsought, by the military-industrial complex. The potential for the disastrous rise of misplaced power exists, and will persist." - President Eisenhower

The disastrous rise of misplaced power certainly has persisted.

Changing politics worldwide

As powerful corporations have entered the global arena, so has politics. Recently, after the Great Recession (which in the US lasted from 2008-2009 and had repercussions years afterwards) many countries have seen the rise of dictators and authoritarians.

Companies that cater to right-wing ideas have done well from the shift. Many companies are now multinational. They may have arisen in one country but they may now be headquartered in another and have workers in many others. A few global companies dominate their industries, having merged with or acquired competitors.

Rise of controlled markets

We touched on the stock market earlier, but it's not a restricted or "controlled" market. Mostly. Controlled markets limit who can enter the market and what prices they can charge. This can be done by regulation, but it can also be done simply by market forces and lack of regulation.

When a handful of companies are allowed to grow very large in a single market and dominate it, they then become very difficult for other companies to enter because the price of entry is too high. The prices that are charged can also become too high. Consider the US healthcare market. It's dominated by a few healthcare players and pharmaceutical companies. Insulin, which is a life-saving medicine, jumped in price so that ordinary Americans could not afford it since there were no companies that would undercut the price.

In a controlled market economy, the government (or other leadership group) tries to direct where money goes. This is often in their own pockets. It's not an altruistic situation. Russia under Vladimir Putin, where money is directed to specific oligarchs (typically oilmen) is a controlled market economy.

Government contracts may be taken away or denied

to perceived enemies of the administration in a controlled market. Attempts are often made to glorify one industry at the expense of another, when one is particularly tied to members of the government. When all industries contribute to the health of the economy, that may not be so bad. However, in a controlled market, industries that make more money and employ more people may lose out to the ones who have friends in the administration.

In such economies and markets, those who flatter and glorify the leaders are the ones who benefit from the control. Those who benefit are already wealthy, or else the leaders wouldn't be able to see and recognize their flattering. Consumers lose, because they're forced to pay the higher prices demanded by the companies and organizations in control.

Chapter Summary

- It's important to know who profits from destroying the environment and harming humanity.
- Technology designed for warfare captures

profits for the contractors who use them and for the politicians who are bought.
- The rise of global multi-nationals has fed a changing political scene across the globe.
- The use of controlled markets is rising, whether they're controlled by the companies that run it or by regulation designed to profit leaders at the expense of citizens.
- One hack: keep tabs on those who profit from immoral activities.

In the next chapter, you will learn about critical thinking and using it in your life.

CHAPTER SIX: WHAT IS CRITICAL THINKING AND HOW CAN YOU DEVELOP IT?

Now that we've discussed how companies compete for our attention and profit from war and environmental destruction, it's time to start thinking about how to counter the zombification that makes them so much money. The first thing to do, which isn't necessarily taught in schools (especially for school districts that teach only to the test), is to use your critical thinking skills. Not sure what they are or if you have them? This book has you covered! And if you already know a bit about it, you'll learn to sharpen the skills you already have.

What is critical thinking?

Briefly, it's the ability to consider a topic clearly and rationally; to logically determine what to do or believe. You take an objective look at it, examining it from all angles. It's independent thinking, because you're not relying on what someone else says to do or think.

A critical thinker can solve problems rationally. They see the connections between arguments, and can both build and assess those arguments. They'll find inconsistencies in reasoning, including their own. Critical thinkers also reflect on their own beliefs and values. They can sort ideas in order of importance and relevance.

You might be wondering why it's so important to be a critical thinker. The zombification in our culture relies on people who don't, won't or can't think for themselves. Those who are willing to consume any kind of information, no matter where it comes from.

For example, there are "studies" out there that claim either that climate change isn't happening, or that it's not man made, and therefore we can do nothing about it. If you're a passive consumer of information like this, that might be the end of it. Maybe you know that more studies are showing that climate change is happening and it's caused by humans.

Maybe you don't know that. Or, maybe you can't tell which side has more science on its side, and you think it's just the equivalent of a he-said, she-said type argument. Especially if one side, the denial side, has all the money. You see many more ads about the lack of climate change and assume that must mean that climate change isn't a thing.

A critical thinker, on the other hand, would see the two sides and if they weren't already familiar with the research, do some of their own. They would look at the scientific studies behind each side. More importantly, perhaps, who paid for those studies.

And they would ask themselves, as we asked in the last chapter, Cui bono? Who benefits? Are those climate denial studies backed by the fossil fuel industry, which has a vested interest in ignoring climate change? (Yes.) Who funded the climate change side? Universities? Governments?

There's another type of zombie out there, who lives in a world of "false equivalence." Decisions are made without considering the credibility of either side. Often, one party in the situation has more credibility and more data than the other, but it's too much work to determine whether that's the case. Sit back in your recliner and have another beer. That is a way to live, but not one that's going to bring you the life you want.

Critical thinking is not necessarily negating the conventional wisdom either. Once you master critical thinking, you will probably find that conventional wisdom is sometimes right and sometimes wrong. It's not the case that large groups of people are always wrong. Working with others can bring you more accurate results!

In other words, critical thinking isn't about being contrary. You can't just rely on the correct answer being that everyone else is wrong and leave it at that. Automatically being contrary is a kind of zombification itself.

Do you want to be a zombie? If you did, you wouldn't be reading this book! Avoid all forms of zombification. If you're not already familiar with critical thinking, here are the basic steps.

1. Identify the problem

What is it you're working on? In the example above, it might be that you're trying to figure out if climate change is real and what the consequences are if it is.

1. Gather information

The Internet is a huge help to critical thinkers (though it can also be a huge hindrance). You can probably find sources for all the different sides of the problem just by doing a few simple searches online. Make sure that you're looking at all the different viewpoints, because if you select just one, your reasoning will be flawed.

For the climate change problem, you'd want to find sources that argue both for and against it being real, and different sources that discuss the consequences. You might try to find some that argue the consequences will be huge and disastrous; some that argue the consequences are either negligible or easily contained; and some that argue the consequences will be huge and beneficial. In other words, all the various responses that you can find.

1. Question the assumptions

Are your sources unbiased, and did your search have bias? If so, go back and try again.

If the only search you did was "how climate change helps the earth", you're probably going to see only one side of the story. If you're trying to learn about love and the only source you used was a pick-up artist forum, your results are going to be extremely biased.

Do this gut-check before you start analyzing so you can do more searches if necessary.

1. Analyze and evaluate the info

We'll discuss the analysis in more detail a little later, but here's where you look at who's funding the research. What arguments are being made? Do some sources make a lot of fallacious arguments, like straw-man (beating up on an argument that the other side doesn't make) or attacking the character of their opponents instead of focusing on the ideas?

When you find a lot of fallacious attacks, that's usually because they don't have very good arguments on their side so they have to attack the other.

1. What's significant?

If you spread your data-gathering net wide enough, you'll probably find many sources and plenty of different arguments about the issue you're studying.

What's significant? What pieces of data are more important than others? Are the pieces relevant to your study?

In the climate change example, who funds the climate deniers is significant. It may also be significant that in many cases they're the same people who made and funded the argument that cigarettes were safe, even though internal tobacco company studies showed that wasn't true.

Peer-reviewed studies on climate change by climate scientists are relevant, spotty studies made by scientists not involved in the field probably aren't significant. The tussle between conservatives and liberals about eating hamburgers isn't. Etc.

1. Find a conclusion

Time for independent thought! You've done your due diligence and determined what's significant and what isn't. Draw your conclusions based on the information available to you. Weigh your conclusions to make sure they're supported by logical arguments and science where applicable. Consider the limitations of the available options, where necessary.

You may end up presenting your conclusion to others, or it may just be something that you need for yourself.

Powerful analysis, and how to use it

Analysis is a key piece of critical thinking. Weighing the evidence, understanding what it means, and recognizing patterns are all important in analysis. When you analyze, you're breaking something apart to understand the components of it. Identify the arguments that are being made and evaluate them. It's the ability to gather and process information on the topic you're working on.

It's key to understand that analysis is objective. If you come in with a bias, you're not analyzing so much as you're just trying to shore up your own beliefs. Look at the problem objectively. What do the different sources say? Are some more credible than others? For example, some websites are known for "fake news" and others for relatively fair reporting. When you rely on biased sources, you're biasing your analysis.

When you're analyzing something, you should be skeptical of all the sides involved in the data you've collected. We all have biases. Good analysis will acknowledge them and spot them. Organize the information by figuring out the main ideas and concepts. Have a neutral mindset. You're asking questions and looking at the consequences of the arguments being made.

Are there any trends in the information, any patterns? Anything that you can tie in to your existing knowledge base? What are the themes? When you compare two pieces of information, what do you see? What insights come up as you compare and contrast?

Beware the human brain's tendency toward what's known as confirmation bias. Our brains like us to be right! We automatically filter information out if it counters what we believe, and we rely on information that supports our belief.

In the climate change example, ideally you'd think to yourself that you're not sure whether it's happening and man-made, and you're going to analyze the information to find out whether it is.

Once you see the scientific studies that all say the same thing, and the logical fallacies made pretty consistently by the deniers, you'll quickly conclude that climate change is anthropogenic (man-made) and indeed is occurring. (Then the question becomes what to do about it, which is an entirely different analysis.)

Why should you spend all this time analyzing information? For one thing, it keeps your skills sharp. Like many skills, critical thinking is use-it-or-lose-it. When you passively accept what authorities tell you all of the time, your thinking gets rusty. Keep it sharp instead.

It's also important for you as a person to think for yourself. It's becoming rarer and rarer, though companies want it more and more. Critical thinking is a hugely marketable skill, as the number of people who can do it declines.

Personal development and the life that you want to lead are dependent on your ability to think independently. You need to be able to apply your analysis skills to where you are now, before you can make a plan to get to where you want to go. Each person's journey is different, so you need to be able to figure out your plan. Otherwise you'll end up using someone else's, and who knows where they want to go!

The benefits of working with a team

Okay, we just got done talking about how important it is to think independently. So why are we now talking about teamwork?

Teams work better when they're full of people who think for themselves. That means that everyone's bringing their own, varied experiences and knowledge to the project, which means there's a better chance of solving the problem efficiently and creatively.

Having a whole bunch of people guess how many jellybeans are in a jar gets you pretty close to the true number when you average out the guesses. Even though each guess is usually wrong.

Collaborative learning brings better results and a better understanding of the topic, which helps in your critical thinking. It brings different perspectives to the problem, which can help you clarify your thinking.

Power of observation

Sometimes it's helpful to be like Sherlock Holmes, with his famed powers of observation and deduction. It's an incredibly valuable skill to be able to quickly read a situation and assess it. Watch for cues and be able to respond to them in a way that's to your advantage. It will also help you in your mission to improve critical thinking, by noticing details that may be significant to your analysis.

It's all about being mindful of your surroundings. How many times have you wandered into the kitchen and forgotten why you came? Do you ever get in the car and reach your destination before you know it, not even knowing how you got there? Dropped a cup because you didn't quite grab it the right way? Stumbled up or down the stairs?

It's usually because your mind is elsewhere. Some people have bad proprioception (the concept of where your body is in space), but mostly it's just that you were thinking about something else so you didn't pay enough attention to your environment.

Being Sherlock just requires you to stop thinking about other things when you're doing something. There are many ways that you can build the habit of being mindful in your activities. Then, it'll be second nature for you to observe things that are related to topics you want to think about critically.

1. Take a daily task and pay attention to it

If you're washing dishes, look at the bubbles from the soap you're using. Smell the fragrance of the soap. Notice how the texture of the dish changes when you scrub off the food bits and rinse it clean.

Or, when you're brushing your teeth, feel the bristles against your teeth and gums. Make sure every tooth gets the care it needs. Etc. See what you can notice about the most ordinary and mundane daily tasks

2. Make "field notes" throughout the day

Scientists do this when they're out in the field. Write down and draw pictures of what you see throughout the day. You'll learn to train your attention on these details. Again, it's good to pick everyday types of things. People drinking water. People browsing in a store. Drivers going by in their cars. Get used to noting down all the fiddly little details.

3. Give yourself a monthly (or daily) noticing challenge

Anything that makes you slow down and pay attention. Maybe you decide to closely look at a new piece of art or a poem every week. Observe the colors of a coworker's outfit every day. Look at the fountain in the square at the same time every day and see if you can spot any differences.

4. Ask questions and be curious about all kinds of things

A great way to be mindful is to remember how you felt as a kid when the world was huge and wonderful. Why do cats have those faces? How does a goat know where to graze every day? How did the moon get those visible details?

Rather than taking a deep dive into one specific knowledge silo, investigate all kinds of things. Sports, arts, reading, music, theatre, science, math, languages... The list is long of all the possible topics out there! Keep your knowledge broad and find out a little bit about various subjects.

5. Connect ideas from your observations and your experience

What things tie into what you already know? It's even better if the ideas in your head and the things you see are different subjects. You might read something about electronics that reminds you of something you learned in music class as a kid. The more connections you can draw, the more patterns you can find, the better your deduction and critical thinking skills will be.

Evaluating situations and reasoning

After you've honed your powers of observation (or while you're learning to observe like Sherlock) it's also important to learn how to evaluate the situation. How strong is the argument, and how strong is the reasoning behind the argument?

As mentioned earlier, people frequently use logical fallacies when they can't make an argument on the merits. When you see logical fallacies instead of logic, you're often dealing with a very weak argument! We discussed the use of a "strawman" but there are plenty of others!

- Ad hominem

It's Latin for "against the man," and that's exactly what it is. Rather than discuss the merits of the argument, the debater makes personal attacks on the other person, or rejects the argument based on the person, not on the argument.

For example, rather than trying to rebut the specifics of a plan, the opposition resorts to name-calling or dredging up personal histories that aren't relevant to the issue, or comment on someone's appearance instead of their policies or experience.

- No true Scotsman

This happens a lot in religious arguments. The defender of some group specifically excludes any counter-examples, to argue for the purity of the group. For example, a Christian faced with evidence of Christians doing something bad would say that "No true Christian" would do those bad things. Therefore the bad Christians are not "true Christians."

- Slippery slope

The argument that once you allow x, you must then allow y and then you're sliding on down the hill to hell in your handbasket. Once you start looking, you'll find plenty of examples of this!

Maybe you're late to work by ten minutes, and your supervisor gets very angry about it. You've been late to work by ten minutes, next time it'll be half an hour, and before you know it, you'll never show up for work.

- Appeal to authority

Claiming that an authority backs you up is a pretty common logical fallacy, especially depending on the authority that you're citing! Typically when someone's appealing to authority either the authority is irrelevant, poor or false.

For example, some scientists have no involvement with any of the climate-based scientists who say that man-made climate change is a hoax. They're irrelevant authorities because their credentials are irrelevant.

And authorities can be wrong. Galileo was excommunicated because the authorities were wrong about the solar system and he was right, though they didn't want to admit they were wrong.

- False dilemma/false dichotomy

The argument here falsely limits the options to two, when in fact there are other options available. It's a way to make one side seem like the hero, and demonize the other. Which is why it's so frequently used by politicians.

It's not just politicians who use it. Kids are experts at it too. "If you don't buy me this book then you don't think reading is important."

Forming a judgment

Now that you've evaluated and analyzed your information, you've studied the arguments and determined where there were biases and logical fallacies, you're ready to render your decision. A good decision is based on the facts and information that you've gathered and analyzed. It may or may not be the same thing you thought it might be when you began the whole process!

Look at the consequences of the judgment as well, when you're evaluating your options. This may affect the conclusions that you draw. One way to test if your conclusion is correct (or at least, probably right) is to ask yourself what you would see if your judgment was wrong, and see if you can find any evidence to support that opposite case. Ask what reasons would make your judgment wrong, and evaluate those reasons.

Suppose, in the climate change example, you concluded that climate change is not happening. You then might ask yourself what you might see if you're wrong. Since those who say it is changing point to warmer than average temperatures and increased storm intensity, you would go back through your information to see if the earth had been experiencing warmer temperatures and more savage storms.

Why is it important to be able to form judgments and test them? If you never draw any conclusions, then what is the point of all the analysis? You could have spent that time doing something else instead.

Being able to stake a claim is sometimes an act of bravery. If everyone you know dismisses climate change as a hoax, it's going to be harder for you to announce that you've done the research and found that actually, it's not a hoax and that something needs to be done about it.

Sticking to your guns is a trait you're going to need to lead the life you want. There's a lot of pressure in various places to just shut up, sit in your recliner, drink your beer and not think about these things.

However, outside pressure to be a zombie still leaves you a zombie, unless you resist it.

You need to be able to test your conclusions because no one gets it right all of the time. Realizing that you're wrong is a key component of learning. You don't want to stick to something wrong. Just because you didn't want to test your conclusions, or you wanted to be done with the project and move on, or you just want to be right.

All these things happen. We're human! The crucial part of staying human is to realize when you're wrong, admit to it, and adapt to the truth. It's hard, and a lot of people don't or won't do it. You will be in a special group if you can let the evidence lead you to the truth and state that you were wrong on the occasions that you are wrong.

Chapter Summary

- Critical thinking is a key component to making sure you don't end up an unthinking zombie.
- Analysis is an important part of the process, as is evaluating the arguments and understanding logical fallacies.

- The power of observation is a Sherlock Holmes skill that you can develop by being more mindful as you go about your daily life.
- Drawing conclusions is necessary for being an independent thinker, and being brave is necessary for not only critical thinking but leading the life you want.
- One simple hack: regularly take a mundane daily task and be completely aware and present for the entire process to improve observation skills.

In the next chapter, you will learn why it's so hard to make something out of your self-education and taking action on it.

CHAPTER SEVEN: WHAT MAKES SELF-EDUCATION, CONTEMPLATION, FOCUS AND TAKING ACTION SO DIFFICULT?

You may have tried a similar journey to leading your ideal life before reading this book. Nothing worked, even if the ideas sounded good and the action steps were laid out. Sometimes it's very difficult just to get started on any kind of path that's different from your current habits and routines, but why is it so hard to focus on doing what you know you should be doing? Why is reflecting honestly on life such a big task? Once you've learned about a course of action, what are the obstacles holding you back from starting?

Self-defeating loop

We're all creatures of habits. There's a certain soothing quality to doing the same thing regularly. Also, once we have a habit for something in place, then we don't need to constantly revisit that decision. If we've developed good habits, that's great. Suppose you got into a habit of working out in the morning after you drink a glass of water.

Both are good, healthy habits! You don't have to think about whether you're going to drink your water in the morning, or whether you're going to work out that day. They're just things you do, like brushing your teeth and washing your face at night (also good habits), packing your lunch and setting out your outfit the night before.

Our brains succumb to "decision fatigue," which is exactly what it sounds like. The more decisions we ask our brains to make, the less willpower we have. Switching tasks drains willpower and focus, a little bit at a time. Many people in Silicon Valley wear the same thing every day (Steve Jobs and his black turtlenecks) and eat the same thing every day, because it cuts down on the need to make decisions. You can save your focus and decision-making reserves for important choices, rather than eroding them little by little on unimportant ones.

You can see why building (good) habits is so important. They also save you time, which is a commodity most modern people need more of!

The problem, of course, is that we also accumulate bad habits. Habits are hard to break. Stopping the bad habit cold generally doesn't work, because in times of stress or boredom you're going to pick that habit right back up! Research shows that habits are loops composed of the following phases: cue-habit-reward.

Rather than trying to break the habit completely, if you want to change your bad habit, you have to recognize the cues as well as the rewards, then replace the habit and rewards parts of the loop.

Suppose you're an emotional eater and you reach for junk food when you get stressed out. The cue is feeling stressed, the habit is eating junk food, and the reward is the temporary numbness from emotional pain, or the rush when the sugar hits your bloodstream.

Want to stop emotional eating? You need to recognize when you get stressed out. Then select a different activity when that happens: call a friend, journal, hit the batting cage, run a mile, whatever it is. When you're starting to implant the habit, you can provide yourself a (nonfood) reward, like listening to your favorite podcast or buying new workout gear. The reward can also just be the endorphins that you get from the positive activity itself.

What happens when you don't do this and try to break your bad habit out of sheer willpower? Well, willpower is pretty similar to a muscle. You can exercise it and build it up, and also you can wear it out. Most people have bad habits in response to something like stress or boredom, and those things happen in modern life! The cues are probably not going to go away. Although, if you don't have a habit to replace your bad habit, the bad one will just slide right back in.

Then you'll feel bad about yourself, because you failed in your goal. That will stress you out, cueing you up again… it's a self-defeating loop. And it happens over and over again, not necessarily because you're weak, but because you just didn't know how to work out the habit loop and replace the bad habit and its reward with a good one and its reward.

Incomplete and indulgent

Most of us don't have everything we need emotionally in life. There's a lack of something, a void within us that we try to fill. With lovers, friends, addictions, activities and so on. The void leaves us searching for something and most of the time we don't even know what it is we're looking for!

Modern life is stressful. We work much more than previous generations did. In most families, both parents must work to pay the bills. Some of this is due to consumerism. But some of it is the fact that wages have stagnated since the 1970s in inflation-adjusted terms. Originally, technology's productivity gains were believed to bring more leisure to Americans.

Instead, the fact that we're tethered to our phones means we're always working. Most people need to put their phones away, to minimize distractions and also to stop working once in a while! Not only does too much work lead to burnout, but research shows that we're only capable of a few hours of intensive brain-work each day. The hours you work beyond that are poor quality and likely to be laden with mistakes.

However, now that fewer Americans are covered by the protections of labor unions, many people are at the mercy of their employers who measure efficiency and productivity, not how well their employees' health is holding up.

The upshot of all this is that many Americans work too many hours and are very tired when they get home from their jobs. We all have plenty of responsibilities between work and home. So it's not exactly a surprise that many of us need an indulgence or three when we get home from work. Chilling in front of the screen, overdrinking and overeating are all ways to indulge that are pretty easy.

Unfortunately, that comes at a cost. You're not really indulging yourself, because your brain and body would actually prefer that you do something that keeps them both active and that you enjoy. Especially if you work at a desk all day. Watching TV, consuming packaged foods and beverages just means that you're tying yourself closer into consumer products and their ads. (In Chapter 10 we'll talk more about how to create good habits.)

This sense of feeling too busy to do anything but slouch in front of something mindless prevents people from learning and growing. You're not going to fail at staring blankly at pictures moving on a screen, but when you start a new hobby or activity, you're probably not going to be very good at it. You anticipate your potential failure and never start anything new, which prevents growth.

Worry, fear and frustration... but no action

Got debt? You're not alone. The tax breaks given to homeowners as well as societal pressure mean that most married couples feel pressure to own a home. Even if it's not financially advisable. Having a home for the vast majority of Americans means mortgage debt. The younger generations have also faced rising college costs in conjunction with wage stagnation, so they often carry student loan debt for decades. Not to mention credit card debt.

All this debt makes people more dependent on their jobs because they require dependable income to pay off the loans and are less willing to speak out or to ask for time off, for fear of losing the job entirely.

If you're extremely poor, you can get (affordable) healthcare in the form of Medicaid, and if you're over 65 you can get (mostly) affordable healthcare with Medicare. Between those two extremes, though, you have coverage through your employer which may or may not be particularly affordable, and only if you're a full-time employee, which means that many people are dependent on their jobs if they get sick.

No wonder people are worried and fearful! If they lose their jobs, they could end up in serious trouble. Even if they have jobs, their budgets may be stretched thin.

Fear is also quite common when trying something new. You may think that you'll never be happy working for someone else, but that job you have comes with healthcare and a steady paycheck no matter how frustrating it is to suck it up whenever you're in the office!

Giving up the benefits to try to be happy is a scary thought for many workers, because when you leave the job, you will lose a steady paycheck, and probably for a while. Employees who want to become entrepreneurs have to save quite a bit of money to support themselves while the business is growing.

Even with the money saved, people find it hard to pull the trigger. You may be in a rut, but ruts are pretty comfy, aren't they? The unknown is scary. Our brains do not like uncertainty. Reality may be hard and inhospitable, but we know what our current reality looks like. Our brains like the certainty of what they know. The future, a different path, is like a leap off a cliff, not knowing if there's water or something soft when you land.

All of which makes it hard to climb out of our ruts. Even when we know we're unhappy, and we're not leading the life we want to lead, we may not know how to get to that life, which is frightening. So, we end up stewing, resentful and frustrated, but not taking any action to change that.

Being distracted, lack of focus and wasting time

Just as indulging yourself with mindless entertainment feels like the easy way out, it also keeps you distracted from reality. Deep down you know you need to be doing something different and better, but whatever that is seems so very far away when your recliner is right in front of you. While you've got the TV on, you might also be playing a game on your phone or scrolling through your social media.

You're not actually doing two things at once. Our culture makes multitasking sound like the most efficient way to get work done, when in fact nothing is farther from the truth. Your brain switches between the tasks, which causes the brain to lose focus and make mistakes. This is also why you should never text and drive. No matter what you believe to be true, the actual facts on the ground are that your brain is switching between the two and making you worse at both.

As a reminder, it takes about 25 minutes to regain focus on a task once you're interrupted. We discussed this earlier in the context of cellphones, but it can be any type of interruption: a coworker coming by to talk, something on TV that makes you look up and pay attention to the screen, etc. Many people, because they spend so much time on their cellphones, lose the ability to focus for longer amounts of time.

It may be getting harder and harder for people, but being able to focus for longer periods is becoming more and more important. As knowledge work increases, the ability to sit still and work is crucial. But when you allow yourself to be distracted constantly, with those dopamine-releasing phone notifications and are no longer willing to sit still for five minutes, you're training your brain to lose focus instead of gain it. You're training yourself to be increasingly incapable of deep work.

Having you distracted and unable to focus is great

for the companies that traffic in your attention. They can pop up lots of fun little distractions on websites to get you to buy their widgets. Your brain gets tired, and they know you're not reaching for a carrot stick or celery stalk when your energy is flagging.

No, you're going to reach for a prepackaged good that has been sold to you. A hit of sugar, salt and fat which the food companies know is addictive. Some kind of flavored water or cola drink with plenty of sugar to keep you hooked.

And while you're indulging, it's hard to get good or interesting work done. If you're eating snacks with one hand, you've only got one hand left over to do things. Which means you can't do writing, crafts or hobbies, which your brain would prefer. Your one hand is perfect for clicking the remote or scrolling down in your social media feed.

In addition to indulging just as the prepared food manufacturers want you to, you're now wasting time just as those who want to monetize your eyeballs want you to. Staring at a screen that is replete with ads, each more eye-popping and attention-grabbing than the last.

You're right where they want you. People who

mindlessly consume are the dream audiences for advertisers. You're not doing anything that will get you ahead or closer to your dream life, when you're indulging yourself like this. It's completely understandable, given how hectic our lives are today.

There are two ways to combat indulgence and time-wasting like this. One is to make your life less hectic, so you feel less desire to indulge. You can do this by changing your mindset about what you need from life, and also by taking concrete actions to make it less hectic. Like delegating chores to the kids or hiring someone to take care of them. The other is to develop habits that avoid these types of indulgences, and instead feed your brain with the novelty and learning that it craves.

Chapter Summary

- The structure of modern society makes it hard to take new action, even when we know we should.
- We try to stop our bad habits, but don't understand how to replace them so we fall prey to them, and feel bad about it, which

leads to doing the bad habit again in a self-defeating loop.
- We all have empty spaces that we're trying to fill, and end up indulging ourselves in ways that feel good at the time but don't serve us.
- People have good reason to fear losing their jobs and trying something new, although that's the only way to lead the lives they want.
- Being unfocused and distracted is good for those who want to make money off our attention, but not good for us!
- One simple hack: find a task or chore that you can delegate out to the kids or hire someone and let them handle it.

In the next chapter, we'll discuss the power of mind hacking and why only those who are psychologically relatively stable should attempt it.

CHAPTER EIGHT: WORD OF CAUTION

So far, what we've discussed is mostly external, how the human brain works in terms of reward systems. Who wants to make money off you and how they're doing it. Who benefits from you mindlessly accepting the messages that you see everyday. What structures lead to self-indulgence and the lack of action on steps toward a better life.

The rest of this book is on mind-hacking. How to use what you've learned about the brain to have yours support the life you want to lead. The thing is, some of what you're about to learn is pretty powerful. If you're not careful, you can do some damage to yourself. Which we want you to avoid!

We want this book to help you uncover the life you

want to lead. To help you figure out the steps to get there. We don't want anyone harming themselves in the process.

Not for complex medical conditions

This may not be right for you if you have trauma or have been diagnosed with something like OCD (Obsessive/Compulsive Disorder). Some of the mental exercises may dredge up or trigger past traumas.

We'll also be discussing how to install new habits. This may be difficult for those with OCD or addiction issues if they end up installing habits which should be good but end up too addictive or compulsive. For example, sometimes people want to install a good eating habit but become so compulsive about it that they drive themselves into a condition known as orthorexia. That's when healthy eating turns into an eating disorder.

If you have existing psychiatric conditions, you may want to discuss this with your doctor first, before you go any farther.

Ask for medical help when you need it

You may not begin with a psychiatric disorder, but they can pop up at any time. You may also have some traumas you're entirely aware of that some of the exercises may bring up for you. Again, we don't want you to hurt yourself! Please seek help if you need it.

If you start feeling anxious or depressed, see a physician. Some of them offer fees on sliding scales if you're concerned about being able to afford mental health care. Don't be ashamed. Your brain is a part of your body. Just as you would go see a doctor when you break a foot, you go see a doctor when your brain doesn't seem to be working the way it should.

Also, see someone if you find your good habits are sliding toward addiction. Most mental health professionals say an activity is addicting if it interferes with your normal routines. Suppose you installed the habit of eating good food. That's great.

However, if you get to the point where you get anxious if you have a meal that includes junk food, and you can't enjoy yourself for the meal, or you stop going out with your friends because they always go to a place that has junk food, or your entire day revolves around planning meals, or you get upset or anxious if you plan a meal but the grocery store runs out of one of the ingredients, these are all signs that your healthy habit is becoming addictive. Find a mental health professional to help you work through it.

Bottom line: if things aren't working right, see a doctor as soon as you can. Mental health is just as important as physical health!

Chapter Summary

- The rest of the book is about mind hacks, and because the mind is so powerful, you need to be careful if you have any existing complex medical conditions.
- You may also develop mental health problems in the future, and you'll need to see a medical professional to take care of it.
- One simple hack: remember your brain is a part of your body, and just as there's nothing shameful about getting medical help when you have issues with your physical health, there's nothing shameful

about getting help for your brain when you need it.

In the next chapter, you will learn about the importance of emotional intelligence and being self-aware.

CHAPTER NINE: IMPROVING EMOTIONAL INTELLIGENCE AND SELF-AWARENESS

Emotional intelligence is the ability to understand your emotions and those of other people, and being able to manage them. You may have heard it referred to as "EQ." There are at least three generally recognized components to this

1. Emotional awareness
First, you must be able to name and understand the emotions you're having as they bubble up. You may not have much control over them at the moment; for example, you might feel a flash of anger as someone cuts you off in traffic.

Emotional awareness allows you to recognize the emotion that's occurring. When a person high in EQ gets cut off in traffic and feels the anger, they can say to themselves, I'm feeling angry.

2. Use them for thinking and problem-solving
Some problems require you to avoid emotional entanglement. For example, feeling scared (or greedy) when it comes to your investment portfolio is only going to damage your portfolio because you'll be emotionally compelled to make unnecessary trades.

Nevertheless, with some problems, emotions can help you.

3. Managing emotions
You may not have control over emotions at the moment (though there are some long-term ways to dial down things like frustration and anger), but what you always have control over is your action or response to that emotion. A high EQ type can regulate their own emotions and help others with theirs, too.

In our example, someone who's good at managing their emotions won't react badly when someone cuts them off. They won't honk their horn, flip the bird, or start yelling and screaming. They may say to themselves something like, "That person might be in a hurry because something bad happened. They may be behaving badly because they're having a bad day," and let it go.

What's so important about developing more emotional intelligence?

For one thing, personal and professional success require that you're aware of your emotions and can manage them appropriately. Machines don't do emotional expressions very well. The kinds of jobs that require people skills are going to still be fulfilled by people and not robots.

Those who aren't aware of their emotions don't understand why they lash out at other people for apparently insignificant things. They aren't aware when childhood traumas are triggered by others, which can lead to totally inappropriate emotional displays. They respond to the smallest provocation because they're unable to let things go and manage their emotions.

Does that sound like anyone you'd like to deal with? A colleague who'd be fun to work with? Or a manager who'd make you enjoy coming to work? Of course not. No one wants to be around people who don't regulate themselves well.

This means if you can't regulate yourself, no one is going to want to work with you or for you either. You may have difficulty developing long-term relationships, both personal and business. Customers will find someone else to buy from, and your friends and potential mates won't want to put up with it either.

Please note that emotional regulation is not the same as emotional repression! That doesn't work either. When you try to bury emotions, they'll always come exploding to the surface at the very moment you don't want them to.

A high EQ person isn't repressing. They understand very well the emotions that are running through them at any given time. They also tend to be sensitive to the emotions of others as well, which helps them in both business and personal life. They don't necessarily respond to the emotions they're experiencing, and they can help others who may be running hot to lower their emotional temperature too.

Self-motivation and empathy

Another skill that you'll find very important on your journey is the ability to motivate yourself because, as you know, sometimes life gets hard! You need to be able to get through those times when you want to give up. Plus, businesses want to hire and work with people who are self-starters.

We'll discuss affirmations in more detail in Chapter Fifteen, but having motivators around you physically helps. These might be quotes that keep you going or even a vision board with your goals on it that you can see as you work. Staying positive is a mindset that helps you do things that are new and maybe a bit scary. Having people around you who support you in your quest to escape zombification is key!

Sometimes you just have to take the next step, no matter what it is, even if it's hard or scary. Make sure that you're focused on the process and not the results. No one can predict or control the future, but what you can control are your own actions. Do the work and let the outcomes go.

Track your progress. When things get hard, or you're not feeling so motivated, you can look back and see how much you've done so far. Another way to help you stay motivated is to make an X or some sort of mark for every day that you take action for a specific goal. For example, if you're trying to eat healthy, make an X on the calendar every day you eat healthy. Once you get a streak together, you won't want to break it! Your brain doesn't like broken patterns.

One of the best ways to keep yourself motivated is, strangely enough, to help others. It makes us feel good. It's hardwired into the human brain. Plus, sometimes you can get so involved in improving someone else's life that you end up forgetting about the problems of your own.

Helping others also helps you develop empathy, which is the ability to experience someone else's inner life and emotions. Empathy is a very important skill when working with others, and if you don't come by it naturally, you can improve upon it. Empathy also helps you to understand where other people are coming from. You'll end up a little less judgemental of people who believe differently from you. Then you can work with them better, which suits people well in business as well as life.

Empathetic people set aside their own biases and beliefs and accept others for who they are, flaws and all. (The corollary to this is that you accept yourself, flaws and all!)

The first step in empathy involves your imagination, so you can see what it's like to live life in someone else's shoes. How does their background affect how they see the world? What do their previous experiences mean in their daily life? In other words, how would you feel if you were in their shoes?

The next step is to adjust that a little bit: how do they feel about the situation? Not how you would feel if it was you with all your experience; but what are their actual feelings about what's going on? You'll need to be able to listen sincerely, and show that you care. Probe gently and respectfully. Then you can identify with them, having been in similar situations yourself or in a different situation but feeling those same emotions.

Make sure you understand where they're coming from, and offer them your support. It could just be your availability to listen to what they have to say or what you did in a similar situation and how it turned out. No advice-giving though—no one wants to hear it!

Self-regulation and social skills

When you're interacting with a lot of EQ, you're not reacting automatically and defensively to what's being said. You won't always agree with others - and actually, you shouldn't. Because otherwise you're not thinking for yourself, but simply accepting other people's opinions as your own, but your reactions aren't immediate, and you don't let fly with the first thing that comes to your mouth. You take time to think about what was said.

If your initial reaction is strongly negative, think about what's really going on. Are you taking it too personally? Has it triggered something from your previous life that isn't a good memory for you? Chances are you're not talking to someone who's intentionally malicious. How could they know what triggers you?

Some people choose their parents very well (!) and were taught emotional self-regulation as children. Many of us didn't learn this skill in childhood, unfortunately, but we can all learn and improve as adults. You can learn to think before you act, how to bounce back after failure, and to deal with stress. These are all key to managing your emotions and actions appropriately.

Mindfulness (more about this topic in Chapter Eleven) and "cognitive reappraisal" are key to developing better emotional management. Learning to stay in the moment and detach from results are important for mindfulness.

Mindfulness (more about this topic in Chapter Eleven) and "cognitive reappraisal" are key to developing better emotional management. Learning to stay in the moment and detach from results are important for mindfulness.

When you reframe your thoughts to be more positive, or at least more neutral, that's cognitive reappraisal. Many of us have the instinct to think the worst when something doesn't go our way. Reframing the thought to be more reasonable helps prevent you from doing something you might regret, or getting all wound up for nothing.

Suppose you texted a friend and didn't hear back for a couple of days. You might automatically think that they're ghosting you, or that they don't like you anymore, or they think you're a bad person or a bad friend and don't want to talk to you. It's crucial to recognize that you have no idea if any of those things are true, and they're probably not. You're projecting from a small piece of data.

You could easily reframe those thoughts. Maybe your friend is super busy or they lost their phone or forgot to charge it up. People who can reframe in this manner are happier than those who don't.

You have a choice in how to react to events that occur or what people say. Choosing a positive way is always going to be more helpful to you.

Being able to regulate yourself translates into social skills too. You'll ask questions to make sure that you understand what the other person means, so there are fewer misunderstandings. Because you don't react automatically with anger and defensiveness, people will be more willing to spend time with you and open up to you, allowing you to build deeper relationships with those who support you. Instead of a self-defeating loop, regulating yourself leads to positive, upward spirals.

Self-awareness

Being able to manage your emotions goes hand-in-hand with being self-aware, where you understand your strengths and weaknesses, beliefs, motivations, and emotions, having all this ownership over your feelings and actions also translates into a better understanding of other people.

It's key for your journey to lead your ideal life. If you don't know what drives you and what your passions are, how do you know what kind of life you want to lead? As mentioned earlier, you may not know exactly what your passions are yet. You might need to try some different activities to find out what lights you up, which can change over time as well. As a child, you might have greatly enjoyed painting, but maybe as an adult, you want to try sculpture or even playing an instrument instead.

Knowing what drives you also helps you to stay motivated. If you know it's not about money for you, then trying to bribe yourself with a monetary reward isn't going to work! If you know that you have to help people in order to be satisfied with your life, you now have a direction to head in.

If you don't know what your strengths and weaknesses are, or what your beliefs are (other than the ones your schooling/friends/parents provided), here are steps you can take to increase your self-awareness.

1. Consider yourself objectively
Yes, this is hard to do! Think about (and write down) things that you've accomplished in the past, things that you wish you were better at and what made you happy when you were a kid. This will help you get to know your strengths and weaknesses better.

2. Every night, write down your thoughts and feelings
Writing, not typing, is important. (You shouldn't have your phone in bed with you anyway—it disturbs your sleep and your bedtime routine.) It's the best way to study and learn because there's something about writing by hand that helps your brain encode the learning better.

Get to know what you're thinking and feeling. Sometimes people rush through the day without letting themselves think or feel because they're busy or scared. No one has to see what you're writing but you, so let it rip. That way you'll be more comfortable with your own thoughts and emotions.

Plus, you'll be better able to recognize when you're

in the grips of an emotion if you've been able to process it.

3. Write down your goals and priorities
What is important to you? Sometimes other people (especially at work!) impose their own priorities on you. What are yours? What feels like an important project that will cause you anguish or remorse if you can't work on it?

If you have some big, audacious goals that you want to work on, they may seem unattainable to you right now. And they probably are. Big goals normally come with lots of work to achieve them. However, once you know what those goals are, you can break them into smaller goals and put together plans on how to achieve them.

If you're having difficulty, they might not be the right goals for you. Maybe you've internalized your parents' goals or even your partner's goals for you. Time to go back to your priorities and values and start again.

4. Reflect on yourself daily
No, you don't have to stand in front of the mirror for

an hour every day! But get in the habit of reflecting on your day. What went right, what went wrong? What would you like to work on?

5. Learn mindful habits
Being mindful is the key to success. Building in habits that keep you in the present keeps you on track to your goals. It also helps you to stay emotionally regulated, so that you appreciate the reality of your situation and think before you act.

Meditation is one habit that will increase your mindfulness.

6. Ask friends/colleagues to tell you how you come across to them

Asking others to describe you may feel scary. Nevertheless, in addition to giving you information about yourself that you weren't aware of, it can also help you to deepen your relationships and develop your connections with other people that much more.

While you're asking, make sure that you're open to constructive criticism, that they feel they can be honest with you without you flipping out. You're probably going to hear things you don't particularly want to hear, but that's the point of the exercise: to find out your own blind spots.

You may get some feedback that you're not really sure matches up, but if you're hearing the same issue, consistently, from everyone, then that is a real problem you want to work on.

When everyone is saying to you that they feel you lack empathy, go back to the section on empathy and start working on it! You may feel that you're actually an empathetic person, but the feedback is telling you that you don't show it.

You can also ask your friends and colleagues to let you know when you're exhibiting behavior that you're trying to change. That way you can try to adjust in the moment, and apologize if and when you need to. Sincere apologies go a long way.

7. Set up a system to get feedback at work
Instead of asking for people to describe you as in #6, here you want to get performance-based feedback. You want to know when you're doing poorly and when you're doing well.

This might be a little scary too, to go to your supervisor and announce that you'd like to know when you're messing up, but most will appreciate your efforts to improve and help you work out a system for receiving constructive criticism.

When you receive it, you need to reflect on it and not be defensive. You might find that it helps to journal about what you heard and the steps you'll take in the future.

Chapter Summary

- Having emotional intelligence (EQ) and self-awareness are key to success in both your personal and business lives.
- It's possible to develop self-motivation and empathy for others, even if you're not currently strong in either.
- EQ also involves being able to manage your emotions, which assist you with social skills as well.
- Self-awareness is also important and can be developed and improved over time.
- One simple hack: begin the habit of

journaling at the end of the day, where you reflect on the day, what went well and what you'd like to improve upon.

In the next chapter, we'll discuss neuroplasticity and how to create good habits.

CHAPTER TEN: NEUROPLASTICITY AND GOOD HABITS

When you think about it, the human brain is a pretty amazing and complex organ! There's always a lot going on up there, even when we're sleeping. The great thing about the brain for our purposes is that it can change as we grow and learn. You can install new (good) habits any time you want, as long as you're OK with putting in the work consistently over time.

Neuroscience and neuroplasticity

Until the 1980s, scientists thought that people were born with all the neurons (brain cells) they would ever have. Once a neuron died, that was it. This kind of thinking implies that you can't learn a lot of new things once you're older. You can't teach an old dog new tricks.

Fortunately, for those of us who want to improve and change our lives, that turns out not to be true. Just as other cells elsewhere in the body die and generate, new neurons develop in adult humans too.

Generating new neurons also means that new neural circuits, or pathways, can be generated. In neuroscience, it's commonly said that "Neurons that fire together, wire together." The more a particular circuit or pathway is used, the stronger it becomes. Likewise, sometimes you have to break a connection if you want to stop using that pathway. This is known as "synaptic pruning."

Circuits that aren't used as much get "pruned" by some of the brain's "gardeners," or microglial cells if you want to get technical. Removing these unused circuits gives the brain more space to build other connections.

The pruning and gardening take place while you sleep. That's why people tell you to "sleep on" a hard problem, or why sometimes you wake up in the morning and suddenly you've solved the problem that's been bothering you for a while. Sleep gives the brain time to reinforce the circuits being used (neurons firing and wiring together) and cut back those that aren't.

This is what gives rise to "neuroplasticity." Connections in the brain get stronger or weaker (and may be removed entirely) depending on how often they're used.

Circuits for thoughts and actions that you think and do a lot get stronger over time. This is why cognitive reappraisal is so important: you don't want your catastrophizing thoughts to be the ones that get stronger, which is also why mindset is so important. When you're thinking more optimistic thoughts, the positive circuits are going to get stronger, but if you're constantly thinking about how stuck you are or how you're no good, those are the circuits that grow more powerful over time.

The stronger they get, the harder they are to break or prune back. You want to facilitate strong connections with thoughts and actions that serve you, ones that make you happy, keep you motivated and on the path to the life you want to lead. Spend too much time dwelling on what went wrong, who was to blame and why you never get anything that you want, and you won't get what you want. Your neural circuits are going to hold you back.

Because older people do have more well-used circuits, whether good or bad, their brains are a bit less plastic than those of younger people. This does not mean that you can only get the life you want when you're young! It just may require more effort and more time if you have ingrained circuits you want to use less of.

Neuroplasticity and habits

Now that you know how neural circuits are made, you probably understand why it takes time for new habits to form! The circuit has to be used to get stronger and using it once or twice just won't cut it.

In Chapter Seven, we discussed how to replace bad habits. If you've been performing a bad habit for a while, you've got a very strong neural circuit already happening. Those connections are strong and tight. So, rather than try to break the loop or let it fall into disuse so the microglial gardeners come in to prune it back, you need to change the circuit after the cue. Slide-in new actions and rewards in the loop that you've already formed.

But what if you want to bring in a new, good habit? For example, suppose you want to write a novel in a year. You've determined that you need to write a thousand words a day to complete it in the timeframe. (As a comparison, two pages of this book are the rough equivalent of a thousand words. It may sound like a lot, but it's definitely doable.)

Right now, though, you're not writing any words in a day. Maybe you tried to write two thousand, and you couldn't do it. Or, when you sit down to write, you can do well over a thousand words, but you don't have a daily habit yet.

The great thing about forming a new habit means that once you've implemented it, you don't have to rely on willpower. It'll automate the work, so that's one less decision you have to make and less decision fatigue on a daily basis because you've already made the decision!

When you're starting a habit, you need to start small. It has to be so easy that doing it is almost easier than not doing it. (For some habits, that's harder than others.) Once you've got that small habit working, you can build on it until you get the full habit installed.

To use our novel-writing example, if you don't regularly knock out a thousand words when you sit down to write, then you'll need to work up to that thousand words over time. Even five hundred words (about a page) is too big to start with.

Maybe you start with writing a sentence a day. Or a paragraph, if writing comes a bit easier for you. That's where you'll begin: one sentence a day.

Installing a new habit

You shouldn't try to start two new habits at once! You need to do one at a time, taking the time to install one before you start working on another. It's easiest to work with habits and routines that already exist, and use them to springboard a new habit off of them.

You'll also need to think about when is the best time to do this habit. Mornings are great for exercise and creative work, but maybe that doesn't work for you. Lunch breaks may be the only time you can see a way to carve out some time for a new habit, or in the evening or after work.

Try to choose a time that doesn't cause you additional stress, requires a lot of moving other things around or for everything to go exactly right for it to work.

For example, if you will only be able to do the habit on nights that you get home from work exactly on time and don't have any domestic issues that pop up, you're not going to be able to put that habit into place. Life happens! You need the time to do the habit so that when things come up it doesn't interfere.

Then, once you know the time, choose a habit or routine that you already do daily. For instance, after your morning exercise or yoga practice, when you leave for lunch, after you wash the dinner dishes or brush your teeth. Whatever it is, make that your cue.

You'll probably need to remind yourself to start with, and periodically during the first month when you're cementing in your new habit. Set your alarm, write yourself a note, etc.

In the writing example, suppose you do yoga every morning and fold up your mat when you're finished. You could use the folding up of the mat to be your cue to head to your desk or wherever you're doing your writing.

Or, you're ready for writing after you brush your teeth. Putting your toothbrush away is the cue to getting your butt in the chair. It's all about one sentence or paragraph at a time.

1. Create the habit

What is it that you want to be doing? Writing your sentence every day? Doing yoga? Journaling? Exercising? Reading an inspirational quote or bio?

Remember that whatever it is, keep it small. Write your sentence. If you're new to yoga, the first step in your habit might very well be unrolling the mat, standing on it, and taking a few deep breaths. Once you've done that for a month, you might try adding a pose. Slowly over time, you'll end up with a yoga practice that's exactly as much of a part of your day as brushing your teeth or washing your face.

If you want to start journaling, just like writing, you can start with one sentence, or more if you write a lot but just haven't put together a journaling practice. Nevertheless, even so, you want to start small. If writing a page a day is overwhelming, don't start there! Maybe just one thing you're grateful for every day will give you a good start.

It's pretty common for people who decide to start exercising to go out hard their first few times. Then they usually get burned out or injured in a short period, and if you haven't had a regular exercise program for a long time, don't expect to start where you left off. Your body isn't in the same shape it was when you stopped, even if your weight hasn't changed.

If you were a star college athlete but it's been years since then and you haven't been keeping up with your sport, you're no longer a star. Start small and build on your small successes. You can't run a marathon until you can run a half or 10K. You can't run a 10K until you can run a 5K, and you can't run a 5K without a mile.

When you've got a reading goal, you still have to start small. A page a day, maybe, depending on how fast you read. You're not going to get through a biography of one of the founding fathers in a day, so don't expect to. Just start with a page or so and go from there.

1. Create (or recognize) a reward

Our brains love rewards, so give it a little boost when

you complete your habit. Maybe you've got a favorite podcast or streaming TV show that you'll only watch if you achieved your habit for the day. You don't want to situate your rewards around food, even if your weight isn't a concern.

It's also best to try to steer away from monetary rewards so that you can spend your money investing in yourself instead of buying things. That's not always practical, though. You might want to reward yourself with a new workout outfit once you've exercised for a week or a month in a row. Buy a fun journal to keep yourself going when the old one runs out. Indulge in a yoga or creative class. Etc.

What can you find to motivate yourself? New music for your playlist? A concert? Fun time out?

Of course, satisfaction is also a reward, but when you're actively making yourself uncomfortable in the drive to improve yourself, you may find you need a little something extra to help you to keep going. Make sure your reward is consistent. The best way to install a new habit is to have your brain excited about the habit because it's getting a reward.

Once you've acquired the habits you want, over time you'll need these external rewards less and less, but use them at the beginning to keep you and your brain motivated and on track.

Chapter Summary

- Neuroplasticity is the brain's ability to make new neural connections, strengthen existing pathways, and prune back connections that go unused.
- The ability to generate new neurons and pathways is what makes installing a new habit possible.
- When you perform the habit regularly, the pathways strengthen and it becomes automatic.
- Use the habit loop of cue-habit-reward to acquire new habits that serve you.
- One simple hack: use an existing (good) habit as the cue for the new habit you want to start doing.

In the next chapter, you will learn about the importance of mindfulness.

CHAPTER ELEVEN: STAYING IN THE PRESENT WITH MINDFULNESS

Mindfulness seems to have permanently infiltrated popular culture. There are plenty of apps to help you stay in the present. You can buy journals with mindfulness prompts and find groups on social media about mindfulness and meditation, which we'll discuss in more detail in Chapter Twelve.

Which begs the question: what is mindfulness, exactly, and why should you care about it?

What mindfulness entails

Staying in the present and attending to each moment is being mindful. You're in tune with your environment as well as your thoughts and feelings. You may not be responding or reacting to them, but you recognize them when they come. You're not judging any of the thoughts or feelings you're having, or the environment you're having them in. You're accepting of them and nurturing and gentle with yourself.

Crucial to being mindful is the sense of being in the present. You're not thinking about the past. Not ruminating, or feeling nostalgic for bygone days, or wishing you'd done or said something differently. You're also not projecting into the future. You're not planning or idealizing, or catastrophizing about what will happen if you don't get the job or something else goes wrong. You're in the present moment.

> **"Yesterday's the past, tomorrow's the future, but today is a gift. That's why it's called the present." - Bil Keane**

Sound like a tall order, to be *in the moment*? For some people it is! There are times when you do need to plan for the future and other times when you must reflect on the past to see what you can learn from your experiences. In other words, you can't stay in the present 100% of the time, though it's good practice to do so as much as possible!

Now the question becomes, why is being mindful so important?

There are a number of benefits to a practice of mindfulness that have been shown in the research.

1. Less anxiety and stress

Being mindful and being present in the moment reduces stress and anxiety. This may be because you can't worry about the future and invent pessimistic scenarios while you're being mindful. The brain can only process one emotional state at a time. When you're in acceptance, you can't be stressed and anxious.

Repeated mindfulness work seems to be able to help soothe people on a long-term basis, not just during the times they're practicing mindfulness.

2. The ability to detach from your thoughts and feelings

The tendency to identify with our emotions and thoughts leads us to low self-esteem. If you attach to thoughts such as "I'm not good enough" or "I can't do this," they become self-fulfilling prophecies.

If, however, when those thoughts come you can

detach from them and see them from your "higher self," they can float away without impacting you. Brains come up with thoughts all of the time, and that's (part of) their job. Which doesn't mean the thoughts are accurate in any way.

Being able to see the thoughts as they occur but not pay any attention to them helps reduce stress and anxiety too.

3. Reduced reactivity

When we talked about emotional regulation a couple of chapters ago, we discussed how important it was to recognize the emotions you're having, but not to act on them, to be able to disengage from the emotions so that you can focus on the task at hand. Being mindful and present is a great way to accomplish this.

4. Better ability to manage pain

Mindfulness has been shown to help people who suffer from chronic pain to manage their condition and improve their quality of life.

5. Better relationships

Although people get stressed out when having difficult discussions with their loved ones, stress hormones come down to normal levels more quickly for those who practice mindfulness.

It helps relationships with children too, probably as a result of being less reactive as noted above.

Mindfulness and the brain

The explosion of knowledge about the brain has brought the science of mindfulness into focus. Research shows that mindfulness practice helps dampen the amygdala, which you might recall is the part of the brain responsible for the fight-or-flight reflex. It also increases the pathways between the prefrontal cortex (where we make logical decisions) and the amygdala. In the last chapter, we talked about how neurons that fire together wire together. More connections between the two regions help the prefrontal cortex take over, so our brains can think more rationally.

Specific types of mindfulness practice, such as loving-kindness meditation (discussed in the next chapter) also dampen the amygdala, especially in the presence of suffering. Also, they can activate the circuits for love and positive feelings.

There's a system in the brain called the "default network," which involves different parts of the brain. Scientists aren't sure exactly what parts are involved, but the prefrontal cortex is. This system is a more recent discovery, which was discovered when researchers found a lot of brain activity when their subjects were supposed to be resting.

This group of regions is less active when our minds are focusing or paying attention. The default network becomes more active when the brain isn't paying attention, or when we're daydreaming, remembering memories, or other ways of thinking when we're not specifically trying to think. It's been linked to depression and conditions such as schizophrenia. Mindfulness practice seems to dampen this activity.

Many people think of mindfulness as some kind of woo-woo or mystical experience, and certainly some people practice it that way, but there has been scientific research into how and why it works. If you need evidence for developing a mindfulness practice, you've got it! Now you just need to know how to do it.

Practicing mindfulness

In the next chapter we will spend more time exploring meditation, which is a specific type of mindfulness practice. There are other ways to stay in the moment, however. Including the self-awareness exercise in Chapter Nine where you learned to take a simple daily routine and experience it, noticing every detail.

1. Moving and eating in the moment

Most of us are busy, so we're always trying to do several things at once. When was the last time that you ate something without doing something else, like reading, scrolling, or watching TV at the same time?

Eat a meal without any distractions. Smell the food before you eat it, and appreciate the way it looks on the plate. Chew slowly, actually tasting your food. Don't take another bite or bring your fork back to your mouth until you've chewed and swallowed every mouthful. You can do this with drinks too.

Do you ever walk anywhere without thinking about something else? When you're on your way to the store, you're probably thinking about what you're going to buy. Most of us are somewhere else mentally while we're walking.

Every once in a while, decide to pay attention to your movement. Feel what it's like to lift your foot from the ground and which parts lift first. Feel the connection to the ground when you set it back down.

(There are also specific eating and moving meditations, but you don't have to do them in so much detail if you're simply practicing being in the moment.)

2. Experience your senses

Humans are indeed primarily visual creatures, but make sure you take time to appreciate the other senses. Being outside in nature is a great time to practice mindfulness! Smell the air and flowers, and the aroma of your coffee or tea as you drink it.

Take in the warmth and presence of the sun on your skin. Listen to the birds and insects and animals, and the breeze through the trees. Even when you're in the desert there is plenty of sense experience when you have the right mindset.

3. Feel a beat before taking action

Just pause a moment before you do whatever you're going to do. Pause before you answer the phone. It refreshes you while you're switching tasks, and allows you to be in the present while you're performing each action.

4. Do something you love

It's so easy to get caught up in the moment when your brain is in the flow! The inner critic shuts up for a little bit, and you're not stressed out about the future or worrying about the past. Your brain loves it when you do things you love. It keeps the dopamine coming.

5. Shake it up

Another thing brains are wired to love? Novelty. Changing things up is a signal to the brain to start focusing and paying attention, so it brings you solidly into the present. Travel someplace you've never been before. Try out a new hobby, sport or type of activity. Take a road you're not familiar with or a new route to work.

6. Watch your thoughts and feelings

Watch them, not in the sense of being careful about them, but in the sense of being a disinterested observer. Remember your thoughts are not you.

Watch them come. Oh look, here comes a thought. There it is. Okay, now let it go.

You can surf your emotions. Even cravings will go away if you leave them long enough. Observe the feeling you're having and ride it until it's gone. Then let it go.

The more you practice mindfulness, the easier being a disinterested observer gets (and the less stressed and anxious you'll feel.) It's a bit hard at first simply because most people are used to identifying with and attaching to their emotions. Whether or not you're successful at first doesn't matter, just the attempt to detach and observe is good enough to start.

Chapter Summary

- Mindfulness entails being in the present moment and accepting it, which is important because it's accompanied by benefits like less stress and better relationships with others, especially loved ones.
- Neuroscience backs up the practice of

mindfulness because research has shown how it affects the brain positively.
- In addition to meditation, there are other ways to practice being in the present.
- One simple hack: take time when you're out in nature to experience all of your senses and notice how they feel.

In the next chapter, we'll discuss meditation and how it helps you to discover your inner self.

CHAPTER TWELVE: UNDERSTANDING YOUR INNER SELF WITH MEDITATION

What is meditation, exactly? By now you know it's a form of mindfulness practice. There's a lot of information out there about meditation, but some of it can be misleading. Meditation is training your awareness and observing your thoughts and feelings without judgment, providing you with a healthier perspective. It's not about you making your mind a complete blank, or turning off emotions or ideas.

Overview of ways to meditate

There are plenty of different meditation methods, and you may need to try different ones before you find one that works for you. Most of them focus on repetition, and how you choose to do that is up to you. Online you'll also find plenty of guided meditations, which may help you ease into a regular (daily) practice.

In order to access the benefits of meditation for your brain, it has to be done consistently, preferably at the same time every day. Like any other habit (refer back to Chapter Ten if you need to!), start small. Very few people find they can sit still for 20 minutes at a go to start! Try one or maybe five minutes when you're beginning a practice.

Here are four methods you can consider when first starting out. Any one of them is fine. You'll need to do one consistently for some time before you can judge whether or not it's right for you. And if there's some other form of meditation you're comfortable with, do that one!

1. Mindfulness meditation

Many people are probably familiar with this type, where you're fully present. It's often very hard to just sit and watch thoughts and feelings come and go, so you can also try paying attention to your breath.

Not changing it (and not counting how many you take), just noticing how it feels when air enters your nose, going through your body, and being expelled. Thoughts and emotions will come while you're doing this, so you're not a failure if you keep getting distracted, but when they do come, dismiss them and return to paying attention to your breath.

2. Transcendental meditation

With this method, you'll repeat a mantra (a word or phrase) silently as you sit in a relaxed position. It's intended to help achieve inner peace without having to concentrate or try very hard. The focus on the mantra prevents other thoughts from coming in and staying.

3. Loving-kindness

This method directs warm feelings and well-wishes toward others. Typically you start with statements like, "May I be happy," "May I be well," "May I be safe and free from harm" and "May I be peaceful and at ease." Then you think of someone you love (who's easy to love) and change the "I" to "you." You can do this for other family and friends, changing the pronoun as necessary. Eventually, you work up to people whom you find difficult, and end with "May all beings…"

Surprisingly, although this one may seem more mystical, it does work!

4. Yoga

First, the caveat that not all yoga is meditative! Your class at the gym probably isn't, unless the instructor spends a lot of the session encouraging matching breathing with the postures. You can take classes at a yoga studio as well, and find them online and streaming.

Take control of your mind with meditation

No matter which form you choose, meditation practice helps you take charge of your mind. Rather than react to your thoughts and feelings, you get to choose whether you act on them. You're no longer ruled by them once you're able to observe them from a distance. It's easier for you to ignore or dismiss those consumerist, "keeping up with the Joneses" messages when you can question their validity, instead of mindlessly succumbing to them.

You'll have greater decision-making abilities because it's easier to experience your negative emotions and then let them go, rather than having your mind fogged by them. With regular meditation, you'll find increased creativity too.

Creativity is key to not turning into a zombie! Not everyone paints or writes, but there are plenty of other ways to be creative. No matter how you express it, it's all about your experiences and your perspective on the world. Also, the more time you spend being creative, the less time you'll be on your phone or electronic gadget being exposed to the messages of those who want to sell your attention to make money.

Meditation has also been shown to assist with self-awareness and a better attention span, as well as memory and clarity of thought. In other words, it has tremendous advantages to those who want to control their minds instead of leaving it at the mercy of random thoughts, emotions or, even worse, corporations and advertisers.

Uniting brain, body, and behavior

Consistent meditation provides consistency in thoughts and actions too. Interestingly, the word "yoga" means "unite." Western thought typically separates mind from body, but in fact, they're tied very closely together. Humans have brain cells in their guts! Mental health affects how you feel physically, and vice versa.

Thoughts and feelings can have physical consequences. When you're nervous, you might feel the well-known "butterflies in the stomach" sensation, or you might clench your jaw when you're anxious or angry. Having a temper is known as being "hot-headed" for a reason! Interestingly, people report similar body sensations for various emotions.

Being aware of the bodily sensation can make you aware of the accompanying emotion. When you're wrapped in a blanket, you might feel the warm and fuzzy sensation of being secure. If you can't or don't pay much attention to how your body is feeling, you're missing out on feeling your emotions too. Meditative practice can help you understand your emotional life better, as well as the lives of others.

Paying attention to your breath slows it down, which relaxes your body, which in turn makes you feel less anxious and depressed. Strengthening your mind-body connection reduces stress and produces more positivity.

Chapter Summary

- Meditation is about training your awareness so that you observe without judgment, and there are different methods to achieve this goal.
- Meditation helps you take back control of your mind, away from your thoughts, emotions and advertisers.
- It's also an effective way to strengthen the connection between your mind and body, which helps raise emotional awareness.
- One simple hack: start meditating by closing your eyes and noticing your breath, bringing yourself back to your breath when feelings and thoughts arrive.

In the next chapter, you will learn about the importance of strategic thinking and problem solving.

CHAPTER THIRTEEN: STRATEGIC THINKING, DECISION MAKING AND PROBLEM SOLVING

When you're improving your life and becoming an independent thinker, it's important to learn how to think strategically and solve problems as well. This can help you boost your career, especially when you want to be a leader. Strategic thinkers find connections among people and ideas that aren't obvious to others.

Strategic thinking

If you don't feel that you're already strong in strategic thinking, know that it's a skill you can develop. It helps if you have good EQ or have been working on that too. Here are some additional tips to help you improve.

1. Be a forward thinker with a long-term focus

Just as you've been learning about not being reactive, now you need to move a step past that. See potential opportunities as they arise, and think about what's going to happen in the future. What might be needed? What skills will people be looking for?

When leadership comes to you, what can you say "yes" to? Is it something that will help you and/or the organization in the future?

2. Dedicate thinking time

In order to make those connections, you'll need time to reflect. Here again, consistency is key and regular practice helps you improve.

3. Don't micro-manage

Trying to manage every tiny little detail isn't the trait of a strategic leader. It's tactical. Concentrate on the higher-level overview. Let employees make mistakes without trying to take control.

4. Take risks (more detail about this in Chapter Fourteen)

Safe is not strategic. Sometimes you need to come up with new ideas and try them out.

5. Keep learning

Thinkers know they don't know everything. There's always more to learn. Not just in your own field, but in others as well. Gathering expertise in other areas will help you round out your thinking.

6. Get additional input

Just as with critical thinking, strategic thinking is best with additional ideas. Putting your head together with other smart or knowledgeable people can only help your thoughts to be more effective.

Another way to get additional input is to expose yourself to new and novel ideas. Brains love it, so indulge them by learning about new places. Better yet, visit them! Meeting new people and trying new things will all bring new ideas into your thinking, helping you broaden the connections.

7. Be creative

Thinking linearly doesn't always lead to the best solution. Sometimes you need to work out a problem differently. Trying new things helps here too!

Decision-making

The ultimate benefit of strategic thinking is to help

you make good decisions. There are many ways to improve your decision-making as well, in addition to making your strategic thinking better!

Too many choices makes it more difficult to make decisions. Studies have shown that people not only choose faster when options are more limited, but they end up happier with that choice later. Pop culture supports FOMO (Fear of Missing Out) too, which can make decision-making more difficult and more subject to regrets.

1. Satisfice

What does that mean? "Suffice with what satisfies." Rather than continue to search for the correct type of notepad, pick the one that seems good enough and move on. Most daily decisions aren't all that important, so don't spend so much time on the unimportant ones.

2. Set aside ego and emotions

All that work on self-awareness puts you in good stead when you're making decisions. You've learned to avoid acting on impulse and reacting to your feelings. Pride doesn't help you with decisions either.

Consider the options from a logical perspective and think about them from all perspectives.

3. Give yourself a deadline...

If you allow yourself forever to make a decision, that's how long it will take! Have a timeline and don't exceed it.

4. ... and don't delay

Set aside some time to think through your decisions. It's not just about the immediate consequences, but the second and third order consequences. In other words, the consequences of the consequences.

5. Plan for the worst-case scenario

We always want things to go well, and sometimes may blind ourselves to reality. To prevent the obvious consequences, consider what could go wrong and what happens if it does. Figure out what risks are associated with your options and bear them in mind when you're making the decision.

Problem solving

The great thing about the human brain is that it

likes to solve puzzles and problems. Even if you don't think you're particularly good at mental challenges right now, developing your problem-solving skills makes use of something that your brain is designed to do. You can think of problem-solving as part science and part craft, which is where you bring your own experience and knowledge into the solution.

In general, solving a problem occurs in four phases.

- Understanding the problem - what's the core idea behind it, and what information is there?
- Plan - figure out how to solve it and find the connection between the information you do have and the unknown aspect of it.
- Execute - carry out the plan and see if you can show that your solution is right.
- Lessons learned - add this solution and anything else you learned to your existing body of knowledge.

Neuroscience also provides us some clues to improve problem solving. The vast majority of our brain activity occurs in the unconscious, or subconscious if you're Freudian. Our conscious minds can process about 40 bits of information during the same time period that the unconscious processes 11 million bits. Much of our problem-solving has to occur when we're not consciously thinking about it, sleep is just one of those times.

The modern world has left us stressed, and it's hard to open up to see new possibilities in these conditions. This means no new ideas, and it's probable that your thinking just settles into a loop. When we're trying to solve a problem, we gather information from reading, talking to people, and try to put all this data into a stressed brain. When you're frustrated and stressed, the thoughts just go around and around without getting anywhere or reaching any conclusions.

Once you've gathered all your data, your brain needs to be calm and unstressed. This enables the problem-solving parietal cortex to get fired up and start solving while you're doing other things. Think about the problem, load in all the knowledge you've gathered, and then leave it. Don't stress yourself trying to focus on it after you've spent some time on it already. Go do something else and let your serene, unstressed mind work on it behind the scenes.

Doing things with your hands is a good way to leave the problem alone. You might try gardening or crafts, something that you enjoy, as a way to stay busy so you're not drifting back into worrying about the problem. Working on a different, hard problem (that isn't quite as hard) will give you the answer.

Leaving your unconscious mind alone to solve the problem is a habit that you need to develop. You'll consistently need to walk away from hard problems that you're trying to solve and do something else, rather than trying harder and harder and getting more and more frustrated. Most people think that the way to solve a problem is just to grind it out until you get something, so this might seem unnatural when you start doing it.

One surprising little hack that can help you solve problems is to talk to yourself as you're solving it. You might not want to do this when you're out in public, but talking to oneself helps to reason through the problem.

There are other tricks to help you solve problems.

1. Music and moving around

Music, in conjunction with exercise, stimulates your

brain. Dancing improves your brain's efficiency, no matter whether it's structured dance like ballet, or more improvised like jazz. Yoga, which is a powerful de-stresser, helps people do better on cognitive tests. Fast-moving sports like soccer help train your brain to process and solve problems faster.

2. Logic puzzles

These helps you build up problem-solving skills in a fun way with no pressure.

3. Sleep

Your unconscious needs time to work! Neural pathways get stronger or, if not being used, get pruned altogether. Rapid eye movement (REM sleep) is important for creativity, so make sure you're getting enough zzzs.

4. Collaborate

Working with other people who are strong problem solvers can help you find better ideas and better solutions. Humans are social animals and even introverts need to spend time with other people. What better way than to solve problems together, using all the varied experiences and knowledge in the group?

5. Be distant

Do you often find yourself giving other people advice, but then you can't figure out what to do in your own life? Other people's problems are so easy to solve! You can look at the issue more objectively when it's not personal to you.

When you're trying to solve a problem, try to put some emotional and mental distance between it and you. If your friend or loved one had the same problem, what would you tell them? If you can solve it for them, the solution will probably work for you too.

6. Journal ideas

Having more ideas helps you to bring together those distant connections that are the key to creative problem-solving. Don't wait until you get home to note down whatever ideas come to you during the day (or night).

Putting your thoughts on paper helps you to work through issues much more effectively than letting them stew in your head, too.

Chapter Summary

- Thinking for yourself also involves thinking strategically, and you can get better with this skill.
- Decision-making is another skill which you need in order to live the life you want, and you can improve this one too.
- Problem-solving is something the brain likes to do, and there are a number of ways to be a champion problem solver, including walking away from the problem.
- One simple hack: if you're in private, talk to yourself as you work through a problem because it will make you more effective.

In the next chapter, you will learn about risk-taking, creativity and using your imagination.

CHAPTER FOURTEEN: RISK-TAKING, CREATIVITY AND IMAGINATION

We've talked before about how much the human brain loves novelty. Leverage that to take the kind of risks that lead you to the life you've always dreamed of! It's important not to stay too safe when you want to make changes in your life. Safety is sitting on the recliner all night watching screens. Taking risks is trying out something new and finding that you like it, or maybe even helpful to you in some way. Creativity and imagination are likewise key for finding your new and improved path.

Taking the right risks

Fluctuations in the areas of the brain that release a lot of dopamine affect whether we take risks or not. The theory is that this developed to help humans deal with rapidly changing environments. Pausing before acting can help you make good risk decisions since the fluctuations mean you might make a totally different decision once you've had time to wait and think about it a little more.

Thinking about risks doesn't entail taking them! Many people believe themselves to be risk-averse, but in fact, we take risks all the time. Sometimes we may not even know that we're doing it. Car crashes kill more people than planes do, but does that prevent you from getting in the car and driving?

To land the job you want, or carve out the ideal life, you need to take more risks. Recognize that you're taking them, but do it anyway. Time has an opportunity cost: if you do one thing, you can't also be doing another. When you're sitting in front of your screen and scrolling through social media, you're not creating anything. It may feel safer in terms of not getting rejected when you never show your creations to the world, but it doesn't get you to the creative life you want, either.

The more risks you take, the better you become at assessing them and the less failure or fear blocks you because a few successful risks tell your brain that you are a successful risk-taker. It's then less likely to try to hold you back out of fear.

What blocks people from taking risks that they need to take to achieve their dream life?

- Fear - of rejection, failure, success, hurting other people, embarrassment. The list goes on, but recognize that when you allow fear to stop you, you're not controlling yourself. Your fears are controlling you.
- Irrational needs - for certainty, safety, not feeling guilty. Again, the list goes on! These "needs" are all in your head. If you let them block you, then you're allowing your thoughts and emotions to control you instead of the other way around.
- Perfectionism - ever heard the expression, "The perfect is the enemy of the good"? Sometimes it's better to just start, or launch something instead of waiting until it's perfect. If nothing is ever good enough, you'll never be able to start on your journey. And if you're always deep in the details, you won't see the opportunities out there waiting for you.

- Wanting a guarantee - but in life, there are no guarantees. You're never going to know for certain if a risk will pay off or not. You can do your due diligence, but at some point, you just have to get off the pot and get going.
- Always relying on others - which absolves you of any responsibility. However, to escape zombification, and to lead your own life, you have to take responsibility for it.
- Denial - isn't just a river in Egypt, as they say! This is another way of evading responsibility. In other words, a way of letting other people run your life instead of you.

Smart risk-taking is not gambling. Once you've considered the risk intelligently, you're in a good spot to decide whether the risk is worth taking. Here's what you should consider when evaluating a risk:

1. Think about the risk logically

It's unlikely that either the most positive or the most negative outcomes will occur, but the results are probably somewhere on the spectrum between them. You've learned not to attach yourself to pessimistic thoughts, but you might see whether you can learn from them before you let them go.

Rehearse in your head how the situation might play out, and make sure you're putting some emotional distance in place to help you think through it rationally.

2. What's the expected value?

What do you expect to happen over time, if you took this same risk over and over again? If most of the experiences are expected to be positive, that's a risk you should probably take. If the effects add up negatively, then you need to look elsewhere. No one can forecast the future, so you're not going to know for sure what the value is until you do it, but you can make an educated guess.

3. Chop away at the big goal until you find something manageable

Just as with habits, big risks are overwhelming and seem impossible. Cut it down step-by-step until you get to something easy to do. The big goals get achieved by the smaller goals being consistently completed. The big risk or the big goal can't be achieved until you take the first step. Even the tiniest step counts as long as it moves you forward.

The power of imagination

When you've got a good imagination, you're a better problem-solver, because you can connect different ideas and come up with unexpected solutions. You've also got your built-in anti-zombification weapon! You can imagine worlds that don't exist right now and things to do instead of succumbing to the dreaded social media feed.

Imagination helps you understand other people better as well. It's much easier to put yourself in someone else's shoes when you've got enough imagination to picture what their world must be like.

> "Logic will get you from A to B. Imagination will get you everywhere." - Albert Einstein

There are plenty of entertaining ways to learn to be more imaginative if you think that your ability to dream is a little underdeveloped. Play games, read fiction, meditate, talk to other people and share ideas and fun with them. Get involved in new projects where you can, and learn about new things as much as you can. Exercise, because your imaginative brain needs plenty of oxygen.

Ready for this one? Doodle! You're not trying to draw anything specific (necessarily), just whatever pops into your head. Do it on your commute (if you're not driving) and in meetings (when no one can see.) And stay curious. Why is the sky blue? Why don't cats have thumbs? Ask even silly questions, and then find out the answer. Let yourself be surprised.

Creativity

Some people don't consider themselves creative, because they don't draw or paint. Creativity comes out in lots of different ways. You may have heard of people being left-brained or right-brained... which is junk science. That's not how the mind works, and many different brain regions are involved when you get creative.

Three specific networks get activated during the creative time. One is the executive attention network, which is used when you need to be focused like a laser beam. Typically when you've got a complex problem that requires some heavy thinking artillery. The default network that we discussed earlier plays a role, particularly when thinking about something different from current reality. The salience network determines which region's networks are most important to the task at hand and switches them up according to demand.

When you're in the flow, which is a very creative state, executive attention is diminished. That helps silence the inner critic, which otherwise can completely block creativity. The default and salience networks are more active. The more you're in flow the more creative you'll be.

Creativity, like most of the other topics we've discussed, is a skill that can be developed and improved. Many of the exercises for developing creativity are similar to those for the imagination: collaboration, staying curious, etc. There are some other ways to harness your inner creative juices.

- Learn from other subject areas and industries

Imagination and creativity involve capturing unusual or distant connections. You know by now that the brain loves new things, so take a new industry or subject and research it. Get to know it. You'll probably notice lots of things that are similar to your own, and others that are different. Take notes and play around with comparing and contrasting. Take inspiration from them.

- Do nothing

Do we have to twist your arm for this one? Do nothing means nothing, it doesn't mean scrolling aimlessly through your social media or watching TV. Doing nothing allows your mind to wander without pressure, which often results in interesting new ideas or questions.

- Walk

Exercise is important for your brain in general, but walking specifically boosts creativity. As long as you don't have to pay too much attention to what you're doing, so walking on a busy street during rush hour isn't going to help you as much. Walking brings more oxygen to your brain while at the same time you don't need to focus, which turns down your executive attention network.

- What's the worst, dumbest idea you can think of?

Maybe you're having a hard time coming up with really good ideas. So don't. Come up with the dumbest, most ridiculous things you can think of. It distresses you and your brain. You're not so focused on trying to find a solution that you get frustrated.

Look at your list of crazy bad ideas and look for the advantages in each one. They may be hard to find, but try. You'll often discover that the good ideas start coming back once you begin this exercise!

- Play an instrument

According to Shakespeare, music is the food of love, but it's food for the brain too. Playing an instrument, not just listening to music, also helps boost creativity. Plus it gets you away from mindless entertainment when you have to focus on what your fingers and eyes are doing.

You may have noticed that there are a lot of similarities in things that boost problem-solving, strategic thinking, and creativity and imagination. Even if you think of these as separate entities. We know that there are certain things the brain finds pleasurable, like new things and solving problems. The more different ways you can express this, the more power you're developing with your mind!

Chapter Summary

- We all take risks, though we need to take different and bigger ones to lead the life we want.
- Imagination can be developed in a number of different ways.
- Creativity is also a skill that can be improved, in amusing and entertaining ways as well.
- One simple hack: doodle to allow your mind to wander freely!

In the next chapter, we'll discuss writing goals down and the power of visualizations and affirmations.

CHAPTER FIFTEEN: VISUALIZATION, AFFIRMATIONS AND WRITING DOWN GOALS

Being creative, imaginative, and taking smart risks help you move through your journey to self-actualization. In life, roadblocks occur. As they say, life happens. You can have a very strong and well-thought out plan to get what you want and yet somehow life manages to get in the way! You'll need to adjust, adapt, and keep going.

But how do you do that when the obstacles seem so big and strong? How do you keep the motivation to maintain those good habits you installed, and take time out to develop your thinking and creative skills?

Use your head. Just like your teacher taught you... though probably not in the way your teacher intended! With all the information we have about how the brain works, we now know how to tap into those automatic processes and the things our brains already like. We can harness these brain processes to help us keep going when the roadblock looks immovable and/or we've drained our willpower out.

Visualization

Athletes, especially the elite ones, have used this technique for years. They see, in rich detail, how they land the dismount off the vault, or the basketball swishes through the net from the three-point line, etc. It's no substitute for physical practice, but it makes a tremendous addition to it. The same mind patterns are activated during the activity as when the activity is imagined. (This is why we discussed improving imagination first!)

Mental imagery trains the brain. Turns out the brain can't tell the difference between actually doing something and mentally doing it. Visualization and mental rehearsal impact things like attention, motor control, memory, planning, and perception. All of which are used in the activity when performed physically.

Even if your goal isn't physical, you can use this technique to help you stay afloat when times get tough. Imagine achieving your goal in detail. Not only what it looks like, but what it smells like. What are the sounds you hear? What kinds of things do you taste? How does it feel? Repeat the visualization exercise on a regular basis.

It's best if you do the visualization when you're not stressed out, to allow the brain to fully get the picture. You might need a few minutes of mindfulness meditation to put yourself in the right mood, use some other relaxation technique, or do it right when you wake up and the day's stresses haven't set in yet!

Affirmations

The right mindset is the key to achieving your goals. It's very hard to be successful when part of you is telling you that you can't do it, that you're too old to launch a new business, that no one else has been able to do it, or whatever else your inner critic likes to whisper in your ear.

In the mindfulness chapter, we talked about detaching from your thoughts and letting them float on by. Another way to help manage this is to replace negative thoughts with affirmations.

Your brain can focus only on one thought at a time.

By replacing negative thoughts with positive ones, you drive out the negativity. Regularly practicing positive thoughts strengthens the connections in your brain (recall that neurons that fire together wire together). When the circuits that lead to positive thoughts are stronger, that's where your attention goes. When you're able to ignore the negative thought circuits for long enough, your mind gardeners will come along and prune those circuits.

So, although you can't really control your thoughts, at least in the short term, they just happen and you have to let them go. You can, over time, develop a positive thinking habit and that will lead to more positive thoughts and fewer negative ones. Although when people hear the word "affirmations" they might think of a Saturday Night Live skit, there is actual science behind it.

What is an affirmation? Any positive phrase or statement about yourself. They can be as long as you want, and you can choose to have more than one. Just make sure you don't have so many that you can't remember them because you do need to use them on a regular basis in order for the positive rewiring to take place. You might want to write them down and have them handy, to counteract any negative thoughts you might be having.

Examples of affirmations:

- "Nobody but me decides how I feel."
- "I am a successful person."
- "I trust myself and my own wisdom."
- "I am in charge of my thoughts, and I don't judge myself."

Writing down goals

By now we've discussed the power of writing (by hand) several times. Research has shown that people have better recall with handwritten notes than they do with typed ones. It's also shown that people who write down their goals regularly are 42% more likely to achieve them!

Writing activates areas of the brain that typing may not. We, humans, are visual creatures, so writing goals down means we can see them. When you write them down, you'll feel more urgency to follow through than if you'd simply left them floating around in your brain. It's also a stress reducer, because your brain no longer has to juggle that plate and it's more restful.

Writing them down helps your brain encode them and remember them better. People tend to recall what they've generated better than what other people have generated. When you take notes by hand, or you write down your goals, you're the one generating. (You can't take down a lecture word for word, so you have to paraphrase and decide what's important when you're taking the notes.)

When you write your goals, you can more realistically assess them. Maybe your big goal is, well, big. It needs to be broken down into smaller parts until you get to some manageable steps, just as you did for risks. It'll help you keep track of your successes and failures. The importance of failures will be explained in more detail in Chapter Seventeen, but you need to keep track of them so you can learn what went wrong and keep track of your successes so that you know what went right, to keep you motivated when the going gets tough.

It doesn't matter how or where you write them, just that you do, repeatedly. It's best if you post them in easily accessible places. When the roadblocks pop up and life happens, you'll have a reminder of why you're taking this journey in the first place. That will help you regroup and adapt. And, when you're not sure if you can do it, look back over the progress that you've made and the successes that you've had. Now you have proof that you're a person who can accomplish things!

Chapter Summary

- Visualization is a powerful technique that uses the power of the mind to rehearse success.
- Affirmations help you to stay in a positive mindset by crowding out negative thoughts so you can be optimistic about your journey.
- Writing goals down harnesses the power of writing to help you stay motivated no matter what happens.
- One simple hack: Imagine your success in great detail, including colors, scents, sounds, tastes and feelings.

In the next chapter, you will learn about the importance of positivity in achieving your goals.

CHAPTER SIXTEEN: ATTITUDE OF GRATITUDE

In previous chapters, you probably noticed that we mentioned having a positive attitude. The right mindset is key to achieving your goals. You can't have success unless you believe you can do it. In this chapter, you'll learn more about key ways to ensure you have an attitude of success: gratitude, positive self-image and actualization. These also feed on existing knowledge about how the brain works, so although these may sound mystical and woo-woo (like some of the other topics you learned about!) there's science to back these up as well.

You'll find all kinds of theories out there about how to be successful and how to achieve your goals. When you come across them, put on your critical thinking cap and study them. Many of these ideas are simply vehicles to sell you something. For example, you might hear people talk about the negative impacts of Big Pharma and how it's all about money. Yet in the same breath they praise supplements, which (thanks to a Congressperson who made money off supplements) is unregulated and is also worth $122 billion.

Think critically, even (or especially) when proponents claim that it's being done out of pure generosity. Are they trying to sell you something? Is there hard data to back up their claims? If not, move on. And let's now move on to some science-backed methods of increasing positivity!

Gratitude

Simply put, gratitude is giving (or feeling) thanks for the positive things in life. Acknowledging the positive is shown to increase happiness. In terms of the brain, dopamine, and serotonin, which are two happy chemicals, are released when we express our gratitude and when we receive it.

As you might expect, gratitude has several benefits in addition to making us happy. It helps build and maintain healthy relationships, especially romantic ones; employees and managers who express gratitude at work are more productive and tend to be a part of stronger teams. It triggers the removal or reduction of negative feelings and helps alleviate pain.

Receiving and giving kindness, which includes gratitude, is known to activate the hypothalamus. It's the key for a number of functions, including sleep. Get more zzzs with more gratitude!

As with most of the other skills you've been building, this one can also be improved with regular practice. Some people's brains predispose them to be more grateful than others, but everyone can develop gratitude. Being grateful does change the brain because you're strengthening those positive pathways and neural circuits.

Keeping a journal and regularly writing down a number of things that you're grateful for is one way to build a practice. Try to vary them and come up with different reasons to give thanks. You might even find something to be grateful for in an otherwise difficult experience. Expressing thanks verbally, to partners, friends or colleagues, is also a good way to obtain the benefits. Even sending a little gift or a thank you note provides an immediate lift in mood.

Positive self-image

Having a good self-image doesn't mean that you're egotistical. It involves a realistic view of the world and your strengths and weaknesses. All human beings have flaws, so finding them doesn't mean you're a bad person. Just as you need to believe in yourself to achieve the life you dream of, you need a positive self-image to help you stay motivated. Accepting yourself makes you less judgemental of others and more fun to be around. It'll be easier to attract those who want to support you in your goals. It boosts your well-being, so you'll be able to enjoy the journey to your dreams. Wherever you go, there you are, so be positive about yourself.

Take a self-image inventory, and note the positives. Ask others to describe your positive attributes (if you haven't done so already!) Develop your strengths. Your affirmations from the last chapter will come in handy here, especially when you begin to doubt yourself. A positive self-image helps you keep going even when motivation starts to flag, or obstacles rear their ugly heads.

Many of the methods to develop a strong self-image you've already been working on from previous chapters. Not dwelling on the negative, controlling your emotions, avoiding comparing yourself to others, and being grateful will all help you improve. Stop being a perfectionist! Meditation is another good way to build a positive concept of yourself. The science behind being emotionally healthy also covers the benefits of a positive self-image.

Actualization (manifestation)

The word "manifestation" is used so often that it's hard to separate the popular, mystical use of it from what happens scientifically. Actualization is another way to say it that hasn't been skewed by popular culture. It relates to the mind-body connection, and may be understood through the "placebo effect."

Generally, when researchers test something like a new pill on human subjects, they need a control group that doesn't get the pill. They can compare the outcomes and see if the results between the two groups (if any) are significant. In order not to bias the study, they normally give the control group a pill that looks just like the pill being tested, but doesn't have the new drug in it. This pill that looks like it's active, but isn't, is called the placebo. The idea is that the test subjects don't know if they're receiving the real drug or a placebo.

The interesting thing is that some of the test subjects who receive the placebo get the good results that the test pill was supposed to induce. Even though they didn't get the actual drug, they thought they did and that was enough for them to get better just thinking that they were getting the new drug. That's the placebo effect, and it happens a lot. So much so that many new drugs never make it to market because they're equally or less powerful than a placebo!

That's how powerful our mind is: it has the power to heal just by thinking it has the power to do so. This is how you manifest, or actualize, success: by thinking you have the power to do so. (and regularly thinking it.) There's some junk science out there known as the "Law of Attraction" that states you can have whatever you want just by asking for it, and that's not true. You still have to do the work.

But when you do ask for what you want, you're signaling to your brain to pay attention to whatever it is you've asked for. When you ask your brain to pay attention, or indicate to it that it should pay attention to something, boy, does it ever! It's a cognitive bias hardwired into the brain, known as attentional bias.

That's why after you look for a car, or buy a new one, you will suddenly see the car you've been looking at all over the roads. Your brain didn't know to pay attention to it before, which is why you didn't notice them so much.

It also puts your mind on alert to pay attention to opportunities that may come. If you haven't asked the universe to deliver it, or written about it, opportunities may come and go without you noticing because your brain doesn't know to look out for it.

Ways to help actualize your goals and dreams include asking for them and writing them down. Visualization is also a great way to help actualize your success. When you visualize in detail, your brain has a lot of things that it can pay attention to, and more opportunities for your subconscious to spot.

Your brain will start noticing, both consciously and unconsciously. Paying attention to the positive things in life helps your brain reinforce the positive circuits and bring you closer to your dreams.

Chapter Summary

- A positive mindset is crucial to success, and a regular practice of gratitude produces many benefits.
- Another aspect to the positive mindset is a positive self-image, and ways to develop a strong concept of yourself are also key in regulating your emotions, as detailed in Chapter Nine.
- Actualizing or manifesting your success is due to the mind's ability to make things happen by thinking and paying attention.
- One simple hack: keep a gratitude journal to express what you're grateful for on a regular basis.

In the last chapter, we will talk about the importance of failure.

CHAPTER SEVENTEEN: FIGHTING FRUSTRATION, FAILURES AND SOCIAL PRESSURE

The great thing about designing the life you want to lead is that it looks different from everyone else's. The terrible thing about it... is that it looks different from everyone else's! Most people accept their lives the way they are, scrolling through social media and wondering why they feel so bad about themselves, or accepting popular entertainment and never trying out other hobbies or creative activities, and feel vaguely stuck.

Your dream life is different, and sometimes people feel threatened by something different or they may not understand why you don't want to sit in your recliner after dinner and stream corporate shows for hours. You may feel pressure to do what everyone else is doing. Especially if that was you in the "old days" before you read and started implementing the tips in this book!

On your path to success, sometimes you're going to fail. If you never fail, that means you're not trying hard enough, you're not risking enough, or your goals aren't big enough. Or all three! No one's path to their dreams is perfectly smooth. You're going to stumble, fall, and run across obstacles that seem immovable.

In previous chapters, we've talked about ways you can stay motivated throughout your journey, but another key lesson for anyone trying to improve their lives is that it's important to fail! It's also important to bounce back after you do. So let's talk failure.

Why failure is so important

There are many ways to fail: you might finish your novel and be rejected by an agent or publisher. You might start your own business and never make any money from it. You might not get the interview at the company you've so diligently studied to get into. And so on.

When you were a baby, did you just get up and walk one day? No; you tried and fell. Tried and fell. Rinse and repeat, over and over. But your parents were sure that one day you'd walk, even though you kept falling, because that's what babies do, and that's how they learn to walk.

Everyone seems to forget this when we become adults. Even as kids, we might have been scolded when we failed a test or an assignment, so failure was seen as a negative thing. If you fail at something in your job, your boss doesn't praise you (unless they're incredibly tuned in to recent thinking about the importance of failure!) Most of the time, in adulthood, failure is seen as wrong and bad. No wonder everyone's so afraid of it!

Silicon Valley, on the other hand, has recently woken up to the power of failing. That's because we learn some incredibly important things by failing.

One is that we gain experience. Sometimes when things go right, we don't reflect on them or consider how much luck and good fortune may have played a part. But when we fail, with the right mindset we can reflect on the experience. What went wrong? How can we prevent that next time?

There's no growth without failure. If you never go outside your comfort zone, then you may not fail, but if you stay inside, you can't grow as a person. It's true, some people seem to fail and never learn! However, since you know how to regulate your emotions and can distance yourself from thoughts of failure, you have the capability of learning and growing after you fall.

It's much easier to be kind and compassionate to others when life hasn't been easy for you. If things have been easy for you, you never develop resilience. Then, when something happens, you cannot bounce back. You never learned how to develop resilience because you didn't need to.

However, it's very unlikely that even if you start life with some privilege, that you won't face failure in some way one day. If you've failed before, you know how to get back up and keep going.

The ability to bounce back

Well, how do you develop resilience? Maybe you've just really stretched yourself for the first time and experienced failure. Now what?

- Know that failure is okay

If it helps, read bios and stories about successful

people and how many times they failed but did not give up. If you think of failure as a feature, not a bug, that helps you realize it's perfectly okay to fail.

Everyone does it. The successful people are the ones who get back up, dust themselves off, and keep going. Failure helps you grow into a better person, so turn it around: why wouldn't you want to fail?

- Ignore the haters

Right off the bat, you can probably think of someone in your life who's a big fan of saying "I told you so!" Ignore them. A stopped clock is right twice a day, but that doesn't mean you should pay attention to it. They're the ones staying safe in their living rooms, and you don't want to emulate them.

- Use it to propel you forward

It's all about growth, so use it. What can you learn, how does the experience improve you as a person? How can it improve your thinking? Reflect on the failure without dwelling on it and determine its lessons. Write them down and keep moving forward.

- Review your goals and create the action plan

It's possible your goals weren't clear enough to start, or need revision now that you've had this experience. Consider what might need to be adjusted, and then create (or adapt) your action plan. Spell out the steps, making sure you have ideas about how you'll move forward after future setbacks.

Building a support network

You want to ignore the haters, but surround yourself with people who support you. These will not be the same people who are pressuring you to keep your old ways, not the same people who want you to stop improving, and not the same people who pooh-pooh the ways you're learning how to use your mind to create your dream life.

Your support network will help you resist social pressure. They may be on a similar journey as you and working to improve themselves. They're the ones reading research about how the brain works so they can hack it for their use, instead of letting others control what they pay attention to.

How do you find these people? You're going to have

to take risks! You're also going to give, which as you may recall lights up your brain and let others give to you, so their brains light up and they associate you with positive emotions.

Reach out to those who seem interesting, have experience or knowledge about your field (or related ones), have achieved a similar goal to the one you're working on, or are on a similar journey. This is where the risk-taking comes in, because you may experience rejection. Don't let it get to you, and keep asking. Note that no one likes the word "mentor" anymore, so avoid using that. People are starting to get a little tired of having their brains picked, too.

Host social events and organize informal get-togethers to "talk shop." The people who come to these types of events are often serious about their self-development, and willing to abandon their screens for a while to socialize and acquire knowledge—exactly the kinds of people you'd like to attract to your network. You can join other groups or take classes that involve your goal in some way.

Don't forget supportive old friends. Some may not be, but you may be pleasantly surprised at the people who welcome a chance to do something interesting and goal-oriented.

Give yourself small and measurable goals to achieve the network, such as talking to one person a day or inviting one person each week for coffee. Having the goals makes it less likely that you'll give up after a couple of rejections or even when life starts getting in the way.

Chapter Summary

- Failure is something that many people look down on in our culture, but in fact it's key to your dream life.
- Developing resilience is also important, since after you fail you have to get back up and keep going.
- A good support network can help you stay motivated to continue toward your goals.
- One simple hack: set a small and measurable goal such as talking to one person a day in order to build up your support network.

FINAL WORDS

Now that we know so much more about how the brain works, we can harness it to achieve our goals and the life we've always dreamed of. Unfortunately, that's become harder to do in our current environment.

There are forces in the modern world that focus on making the planet seem chaotic because that's how they make money. Other entities make money off our attention and have designed their apps, feeds, and characteristics to make them addictive so we spend all our time on them. They've harnessed their knowledge of the brain and tried to use our own minds against us.

The modern world also makes it hard for people to make their own way, to buck the system and avoid comparing themselves to the Joneses but also to be confident in themselves. Self-limiting beliefs get reinforced, and social norms police what is appropriate behavior, and where and when.

Not many people think for themselves when it's so easy to fall into the popular narrative and conform. The rise of digital technologies has created even more opportunities for people to be monitored and manipulated. Though the ability to think critically is increasingly in demand, fewer people can actually do it.

Self-education often doesn't work, because people don't understand the fundamental idea underpinning how to take action that works: to work with the brain, and not against it, to use its power for leverage over yourself and to gain control of yourself. In other words, to learn how to hack your brain for your own benefit.

Being in control of one's own mind is important, and it's also incredibly powerful. Enough so that some people are not good candidates for mind hacking, because they might cause harm to themselves instead of improving their lives. Seeing a medical professional is always a good idea when you need help or it seems like things have gone awry in your brain.

With the tools in this book and armed with knowledge about how your brain works, you learned how to regulate your emotions. It's important to be able to act instead of react, not only for your own mental health but also when interacting with other people. Becoming self-aware and then being able to empathize with others are the basics of success. Both professionally and personally.

The brain is able to generate new brain cells (which is a relatively new discovery) and rewire pathways, which is known as neuroplasticity. Circuits that get used more become stronger and those not in use get pruned away. That's why new habits need to be done consistently for a period of time before they're "installed" in the brain. The habit loop consists of three phases: cue-habit-reward. To build new habits, you can build off existing cues. It's hard to break bad habits. Replacing the bad habit after the cue with the good habit, and recognizing the reward, rewires the brain for the good habit.

Being mindful is a good way to stay in the present so that you're neither agonizing over the past nor projecting catastrophes into the future. It helps you detach from your thoughts, so you don't dwell on the negative ones. You learn to watch the thoughts come and go, almost as if they're happening in someone else's brain. Implementing a mindful practice helps you destress and focus on the positive.

Meditation is a form of mindfulness also and trains your brain to be attentive to the right things. You learn to let thoughts and emotions come and go. The connection between your mind, behavior, and body is strengthened with a regular meditation practice. This connection also helps you on your journey to achieve your goals.

Strategic thinking and problem-solving, as well as decision-making, are skills that can be improved through practice. Because our unconscious is actually responsible for most of the brain's activity, leaving a problem to allow the unconscious to work on it is often the best solution, even though it seems counterintuitive to stop working on a problem.

Creativity, the use of the imagination, and risk-taking can all be developed through knowledge of the mind and how it works. Not only do these ideas help you solve problems, but they can also help you stay motivated on your journey.

Having a positive mindset is the key to success. You have to believe you can achieve your goals in order to reach them. You have to know that your journey is possible to start it. There are many aspects to paying attention to the positive.

Among them is the regular practice of visualizing your goals and successes, writing your goals down (by hand!) and developing and using affirmations. Though they may seem mystical in quality, they're all backed by neuroscience. As are practicing gratitude on a regular basis, building a positive self-image, and actualizing (or manifesting) success by thinking about it and asking for it.

Finally, and also maybe unexpectedly, failing is also fundamental to success! Not failing means your dreams aren't big enough and you're playing it too safe. Failing is a feature, not a bug. You learned how to develop resilience and a support network so you can get back up and keep going.

Mind hacking may sound scary, and certainly, you don't want anyone else trying to hack your mind, but by harnessing the power of your mind, you can escape the zombification of staring at screens and passively absorbing what other people want you to consume and pay attention to. Attention is a hot commodity, but you're the one who should be in control of where you put yours.

If you only take away one thing from this book, understand that no matter what's going on externally, your mind gives you the power to get what you want. You can develop the skills you need to lead your dream life, just by understanding how your mind works and putting some simple ideas into regular and consistent practice.

THE END... ALMOST!

Reviews are not easy to come by.

As an independent author with a tiny marketing budget, I rely on readers, like you, to leave a short review on Amazon.

Even if it's just a sentence or two!

THE END... ALMOST!

So if you enjoyed the book, please...

>> **Click here to leave a brief review on Amazon.**

I am very appreciative for your review as it truly makes a difference.

Thank you from the bottom of my heart for purchasing this book and reading it to the end.

www.ingramcontent.com/pod-product-compliance
Lightning Source LLC
Chambersburg PA
CBHW030325100526
44592CB00010B/566